# Crime and the Media

## *Headlines versus Reality*

### Roslyn Muraskin
*Long Island University*

### Shelly Feuer Domash

PEARSON

Prentice
Hall

Upper Saddle River, New Jersey, 07458

Library of Congress Cataloging-in-Publication Data
Muraskin, Roslyn.
   Crime and the media : headlines versus reality / Roslyn Muraskin
and Shelly Feuer Domash.
      p. cm.
   Includes bibliographical references and index.
   ISBN 0-13-192133-9
   1. Crime in mass media. 2. Crime and the press—United States
   —Case studies. 3. Mass media and criminal justice—United States
   —Case studies.   I. Domash, Shelly Feuer.  II. Title.
   P96.C742U66 2007
   364.973—dc22                                             2006016910

Editor-in-Chief: Vernon R. Anthony
Executive Editor: Frank Mortimer, Jr.
Associate Editor: Sarah Holle
Marketing Manager: Adam Kloza
Editorial Assistant: Jillian Allison
Production Editor: Samirendra Ghosh/Techbooks
Production Liaison: Barbara Marttine Cappuccio
Director of Manufacturing and Production: Bruce Johnson
Managing Editor: Mary Carnis
Manufacturing Manager: Ilene Sanford
Manufacturing Buyer: Cathlene Petersen
Senior Design Coordinator: Mary Siener
Cover Designer: Allen Gold
Cover Image: Philippe Ushetto/Getty Images
Composition: Techbooks
Printing and Binding: R. R. Donnelley & Sons

Pearson Education Ltd.                    Pearson Education Australia Pty. Limited
Pearson Education Singapore Pte. Ltd.     Pearson Education North Asia Ltd.
Pearson Education Canada, Ltd.            Pearson Educación de Mexico, S.A. de C.V.
Pearson Education—Japan                   Pearson Education Malaysia Pte. Ltd.

10 9 8 7 6 5 4 3 2 1
ISBN: 0-13-192133-9

This work is dedicated to all those presumed innocent and not found guilty by the media. I give my love and thanks to my family as I pursue the love of learning and writing. Additional thanks to Long Island University for allowing me to explore issues of interest as I continue my research in the field of criminal justice.

Roslyn Muraskin

I dedicate this work to my colleagues in journalism, who showed me the way; to my friends in law enforcement, who showed me a different side of life; and to my family, who showed me why it is all worthwhile.

Shelly Feuer Domash

# Contents

# Preface

The media's handling of criminal incidents has always fascinated me, both as a reader and as an academic. What is it about the media that drives them to write or talk about a particular story and ignore others? Celebrity cases always seem to make front-page news headlines. When a citizen is accused of committing a crime, the decision to report it appears to depend on how newsworthy the story is. We have been conditioned to receive the news as reported and to believe that their version is the way it actually happened. Yet we live in a world where an individual is supposed to be presumed innocent until found guilty, but apparently not by the media.

Our knowledge of crime and justice comes primarily from the media. We have a fascination with crime. What concerns us is whether the coverage of sensational acts affects future victims, and if so, how? By reading the headlines and by watching crime television shows, do we feel more threatened by crime than absolutely necessary? There is a fear of crime, but is the media to be held responsible for such fear?

What this work has set out to do is describe some cases and indicate how the media influences us and impacts our attitudes about crime. We appear to be accepting of crime in our society on an everyday level, yet what should be the focus of the media? Is reporting of crime done fairly? Do the media allow us or persuade us to jump to conclusions about the guilt of arrested individuals?

We look for heroes in our society and yet, when celebrities are arrested for having committed a crime, we are still enamored of their celebrity status. Look at the cases of Michael Jackson and O.J. Simpson (as described in this work). Both are celebrities and today, both are free men, having been acquitted by the courts. The courts have declared that they are innocent. The question in the minds of many and still being discussed is whether each is truly innocent. Did the media influence us in coming to the same conclusion as the jurors?

Who makes the headlines, the media or the criminal? We choose the former. Threats to the status quo must be eliminated, but are we in a rush to judgment?

What exactly are the images of crime and justice as they are presented by the mass media? What kinds of behavior do the media cover? What behavior is ignored by the media? Do the media exaggerate the occurrence of crimes as committed by certain people, while ignoring other crimes? And, if so, why? The public appears to be accepting of crime stories as depicted by the media. The issue that must be discussed is whether the media presents an accurate picture. Or is it true that the media, in order to sell, has to make exceptional headlines? Do we have a stereotypical view of justice formed by the media, or are we well educated as to what truth is? The media helps form our opinions on right and wrong. The public pressure to believe everything that is written or said makes a statement about the role of the media and its influence on the populace. The media "plays" at reporting the news. What we must understand is the accuracy of their reporting. What exactly is the relationship between law and the reporting of it? Do we assume guilt before the person who stands accused is adjudicated by the courts?

Is it myth or reality? Read on.

Roslyn Muraskin

# About the Authors

**Roslyn Muraskin, Ph.D.,** is Professor of Criminal Justice at the C.W. Post Campus of Long Island University. Her published works include *It's a Crime: Women and Justice* (4th ed., 2007, Prentice Hall); *Key Correctional Issues* (2005, Prentice Hall); *Visions for Change: Crime and Justice in the Twenty-First Century* with Albert R. Roberts (2005, Prentice Hall); and is editor of the Women's Series for Prentice Hall. Other publications include "Mothers and Fetuses: Enter the Fetal Police," "Directions for the Future," and "Measuring Disparity in Correctional Facilities." In addition, Dr. Muraskin serves on the Editorial Board of the *Encyclopedia of Criminology* and has written and spoken on numerous topics concerning gender and the law.

Dr. Muraskin serves as the Director of the Long Island Women's Institute for the College of Management at Long Island University, and serves as the Executive Director of the Alumni Chapter for the College of Management. She served in the capacity of Associate Dean of the College of Management (1990–1996) as well as Director of the School of Public Service.

She received her doctorate in criminal justice from the Graduate Center at the City University of New York, and her master's degree at New York University. She received her bachelor's degree from Queens College.

Dr. Muraskin's main research interests are those of gender and the law; in particular, disparities in corrections as well as throughout the criminal justice system. She is a frequent lecturer on issues of gender and a commentator on television and radio.

**Shelly Feuer Domash** is a freelance reporter for the *New York Times, Police Magazine,* and many other national publications. She has extensive experience in radio, televion, and print media. Her career began as the first woman newscaster reporting from Long Island, New York. Ms. Domash then went on to become a production assistant at WABC-TV. She anchored the evening news on WLIW-TV, then produced and anchored her own women's talk show for the station. Her first story for *Newsday* exposed the high incidence of breast cancer on Long Island. Working for the *New York Times,* she specialized in police reporting, feature writing, and investigative and daily news stories. Her interest in independent film projects resulted in numerous documentaries that she produced, directed, and wrote. Her documentary on gangs was the first in-depth look at the impact of gangs on Long Island. Her drug abuse documentary, in addition to being aired on television, was shown daily on tours of the Supreme Court building in Mineola, New York; used as a training tool in high schools; and aired in drug rehabilitation centers in New York State.

Ms. Domash has also worked on the other side of the media, heading the public relations departments for the Nassau County Health Department, New York, and the Town of Hempstead, New York. She has lectured extensively on breast cancer, drugs, gangs, and women's issues. Ms. Domash has received numerous awards for her professional accomplishments, including six press club awards for both her stories in the *New York Times* and her documentaries; the Coalition for Fair Broadcasting awards for two of her documentaries; the Cable Industry's Gilbert Award; and the Nassau County Bar Association award for public service.

## CONTRIBUTOR

**Krista Gehring** received her undergraduate degree from the University of Colorado at Boulder, where she was exposed to the study of crime and justice in courses taught by death penalty scholar Michael Radelet. She has studied with scholars such as James Alan Fox, Nicole Rafter, and Peter Manning. Her areas of interest are media representation of crime, crime and popular culture, sentencing practices, capital punishment, history of corrections, and incarceration rates in America. After receiving her master's degree from Northeastern University, she served as an adjunct faculty member. She is currently an adjunct professor for the University of Northern Colorado, where she teaches undergraduate courses in criminal justice and juvenile delinquency.

# 1

# Overview

## Crime and Media: Headlines versus Reality

### "We interrupt this show to bring you an important announcement!"

How many times do we hear this announcement as we sit back to watch our favorite television show, or hear it on the radio as we drive to or from work? We are a culture greatly influenced by the media. The media has a captive audience: us. The information disseminated is at their discretion. "The cliché phrase, 'if it bleeds, it leads' is unfortunately the case with the American media; the search for heinous, outrageous and even *sexy* crimes, no matter how rare the incident, . . . is sure to boost ratings" (Gehring, 2005).

The public's knowledge of crime is primarily derived from its depiction in the media. The media affects the public's fear of crime, its opinion of punishment, and its perception of the police. If the media is responsible for the headlines, the conclusion is that it influences the public's attitude regarding crime incidents.

Society is mesmerized by the study of crime and justice. We constantly engage in "crime talk" as a result of viewing films; reading books, newspapers, and magazines; watching television (e.g., *Law & Order, CSI Miami, NYPD Blue*); and listening to the news on the radio. There is a fascination with crime reporting. The mass media is where most individuals learn about crime. But is the depiction of crime by the media reality or simply headlines? Who makes the headlines, the media or the criminals?

This text will examine, through the study of cases that have made headlines, the understanding of crime as well as the fear of crime among the populace. The television shows and movies we watch, with all their gore, appear to depict crime "as it really is," or do they? The headlines instill in the masses a fear of crime and a distrust of the entire criminal justice system. In this work, we examine the tenet that crime is portrayed in the media not so much with truth in mind, but rather as a means to excite, upset, and sell the news.

The news media focuses on negative criticism rather than on positive or successful crime prevention efforts. The evolution of American criminal law into what is referred to as "talk-show fodder" has worsened the traditional vitriolic relationship between the defense and the prosecution sides of the criminal justice system. Our system of justice means fairness, but fairness is not always obtained. If we define *justice* as a means of *fairness*, then sensitive information is not always kept from the public. The conclusion is that the influence of the media on our system of justice means gag orders are almost impossible to enforce.

According to *Cyber Rights and Criminal Justice*, which was originally written in 1994, there is little time for shenanigans surrounding the media and the criminal justice system. Headlines make the news and the news is printed with the stories that will sell quickly. There is always a high-profile case that is tried in the media as opposed to the courtroom. This text will demonstrate this factor with examples of cases throughout history right up until the twenty-first century.

"More is at stake than ratings. In their trivialization of criminal procedure, the traditional media have failed us all," Brenner, 2000; (http://avalon.caltech.edu/~thanne/law.html). There is the court of opinion and there is the public court of opinion as influenced by the media. Which one are we to believe? Research indicates that the average citizen obtains close to 96 percent of information regarding crime from the media alone (Kappeler, Blumberg, & Potter, 2000). The problem with this is that the populace accepts the written and reported words with no regard for their source and/or accuracy.

In addition to cases (some of which are described in the following paragraphs), we focus on how laws are applied, the truth about policies, the increased incarceration rates, and the war on drugs in an effort to try to appreciate the factors that influence our understanding of the criminal justice system. We scrutinize to what degree these factors are prompted by the media and reflect a sense of crisis. How extreme is the role of the media and its influence?

Discussed in this work are the images of crime, justice, and the criminal justice system as portrayed by the mass media. In order to grasp the kind of behavior the media covers, we also scrutinize cases that are ignored. We examine if the media goes to enormous lengths to exaggerate the occurrence of some crimes while ignoring others. We study how the media portrays the role of the police, the prosecutors, the defense attorneys, and the judges and juries through an examination of major cases. We need to understand how the media impacts the administration of justice. We will discuss the O.J. Simpson case and assess its influence in the Michael Jackson case. Both men were acquitted of all criminal charges, though civil suits do exist. Do all celebrities go free? They appear not to be immune from prosecution. But then we look at the case of Martha Stewart. Why was she convicted? Do the media perform a fair job in describing the successes and failures of our criminal justice system, or a biased view detrimental to the administration of justice? Are there ways to overcome the stereotypes depicted by the media?

## HIGHLIGHTS OF CASES PRESENTED IN THE PRESS

- Scott Peterson (see Chapter 14) was accused of murdering his wife, Laci, when she was eight months pregnant. He was convicted in 2004 and sentenced to die. The story resulted in a media circus. Even Peterson's alleged mistress held press conferences while hiring a high-powered attorney. We were told that the prosecution decided not to call her at pretrial, but the defense team said they wanted to subpoena her as a witness. The fetus found with Laci's body was named Conner, adding a second victim to the public's sense of outrage; yet the law states that a fetus is not yet a person. The scenes of where Laci's body was discovered were played over and over again, just in case someone was out of the country and missed it.

  There were public disputes over the autopsy results and how the bodies were mutilated. This murder entered the public domain and was tried in the realm of public opinion. We are told Scott Peterson got a fair trial, and yet the media picked this particular case to lead the headlines over and over again.

- The murder of Marilyn Sheppard in 1954 became the basis for a TV series and motion picture. This case received substantial media attention. The pretrial media had her husband, Sam Sheppard, tried and convicted, and the jury followed suit. After he spent ten years in prison, the Supreme Court overturned his conviction, blaming the pretrial publicity.

- The murder of JonBenet Ramsey (see Chapter 10) was particularly appealing to the media. This young child came from a seemingly idyllic American family, comprised of beautiful children and a former beauty queen married to a very successful businessman. Then on Christmas night, 1996, JonBenet was found murdered in the basement of her luxurious home. The Ramseys became quick suspects. They hired a public relations firm to help them with their image. They held press conferences, and books were written. Every media outlet tried for its own angle on this story. The case has not gone to the courts, but has been tried in the court of public opinion by the media. To this day, no one has been tried for this crime. Yet, recent DNA evidence indicates that perhaps it was an intruder—a stranger—who committed the crime, and not a member of the immediate family, as reported by the media.

- Three football players from Merrick, New York, were accused of sexual assault after a hazing incident at a training camp in Pennsylvania. The Memphan High School case rocked the suburban community, resulting in nationwide coverage. A small radical hate group from the Midwest came to protest, and although their group consisted of only five people, they drew nationwide media coverage. Why?

    The weapons in this incident—broomsticks, pine cones, and golf balls—were all used to sodomize three freshman players over three to four days. It was reported that the broomsticks were dipped in Mineral Ice, an ointment that burns those with sensitive skin.

    Meanwhile, the parents and friends of the victims attempted to use the media to force a Pennsylvania judge to try the students as adults; they failed. Eighteen relatives and family friends packed the court but were clearly outnumbered by the media representatives reporting the story. The judge, in his pronouncement that these young people were to be adjudicated as juveniles, ignored public opinion, but that did not stop the media blitz.

- A nine-month trial for a famous defendant ended with a not guilty ruling. O.J. Simpson (see Chapter 9), known for his high-priced and high-powered lawyers, took on the criminal justice system. The prosecutor, Marcia Clark, a woman who changed her hairstyle continually throughout the trial, seemingly playing more to the public than the jury, became a media personality. She later reported for a major television network on the Michael Jackson case as well as other cases.

The O.J. case was the longest trial in the history of California, costing more than $20,000,000. The trial was surrounded by never-ending coverage and never-ending media hype. Research indicated that 74 percent of Americans could identify Kato Kaelin, but only 25 percent knew who Vice President Al Gore was.

Two thousand reporters covered this infamous trial; 121 video feeds snaked out of the building where the trial was held. Twenty-three newspapers and magazines were represented throughout the trial. More than eighty books about the trial have been published. Did the media portray O.J. Simpson as the innocent person he claimed to be, or did Nicole Brown Simpson and Ronald Goldman, the victims, take a back seat? To this day, the question lingers: Did O.J. do it?

- On December 7, 1993, Colin Ferguson (see Chapter 8) took out a gun and opened fire on a group of commuters aboard a Long Island (New York) Railroad commuter train as they were heading home from a day at work. The trial captured the media's attention because Ferguson refused counsel and defended himself. Perhaps one of the more noteworthy parts of this crime is what happened to one victim's relative, Carolyn McCarthy, who had been a nurse. She gained notoriety as the wife of a murdered husband and the mother of an injured son. She took that fame and, running on the platform of gun control, she was elected to Congress. The media made a victim into a heroine. More important, we discover that repeated exposure combined with the sympathy angle can project an image that propels an ordinary citizen into the political arena.

- Elizabeth Smart (see Chapter 13) was taken from her parents' home and was missing for months. Her parents, not happy with the police department investigation, turned to the media for help. It worked. A couple saw a picture of her abductor and recognized Elizabeth walking on the street. The police were called. There were TV movies about the case, and it seemingly forced the president into signing the Amber Alert law. Here, the media played a positive role in identifying Elizabeth Smart on the street and catching her kidnapper.

- Was Andrea Yates, who drowned her five children in 2001, a killer, or a female suffering from postpartum syndrome? The media did not accept such a defense. Rather than being hospitalized, Andrea Yates was to serve time in a correctional facility. The district attorney had wanted her to die by lethal injection. Yet her conviction was overturned due to the fictitious testimony presented by one of the psychiatrists. He claimed she was under the undue influence of the show *Law & Order*, yet the episode she was supposed to have viewed never aired. She remains incarcerated, undergoing treatment. Her husband has since divorced her and has remarried.

Maggie Young drowned her five children in 1965 and was sent to a mental institution. The media was "taken in" by Susan Smith in 1994. Her children were allegedly kidnapped, and then it turned out that she had drowned them by pushing her car into the river. The role of the media in 1965 and in 2001 changed with Andrea Yates.

- Coverage of crimes concerning women and their children suffers from stereotypical portrayals. A woman who suffers from severe hormonal changes can turn around and kill. Who believes that? A woman who has been a victim of domestic violence over many years kills her husband or boyfriend, and uses the defense of battered women's syndrome, a defense of self-defense. There are few who understand this gender defense, a defense available to women who attempt to prove they were or are victims of domestic violence, but then there is the belief factor. But public opinion is that the battered woman should have left her husband a long time ago. When you kill, you are a murderer. It's the victim turning on the victimizer, and the victim is the one to be punished.

- Who is Gary Ridgway, the admitted serial killer of forty-eight females, chased by the law for more than two decades? How do the media portray him and his atrocious acts?

- And then there is the case of Princess Diana's death. What is it about royalty that makes us so curious? We look to the media for answers about her death, and about Prince Charles's former valet, George Smith, who claims to have been raped. The media draws our attention to these cases because of our fascination with royalty.

Who uses the media, and to what extent, and why? We read about the Salem witch trials and find the victims were not really witches at all, but rather groups of rebellious women. Then there is

John Hinckley. The media tells us he is eligible for parole, and the media argues against his release. And others?

Who reports the truth? The media, more than any other source, has the greatest "influence on the perception on crime and criminality" (Jerin & Fields, 2005). According to Jerin and Fields, the media has been used as it was during the mid-seventeenth century through the use of the printed word. According to Surette (1998), the type of publications used during this time "functioned as entertainment for the public using an informational format, which in turn assembled a relationship between crime and the social counterpart of sin" (Jerin & Fields, 2005). In 1953, Davis offered proof that no relationship existed between crime as reported by the media and actual crime statistics. Surette (1998) stated that "crime is seen to be the single most popular story element in the history of U.S. commercial television, with crime-related shows regularly accounting for one-fourth to one-third of all prime-time shows" (in Jerin & Fields, p. 68).

> The television market for illustrating crime has significantly increased over the last few decades. The television era, at one time, could be classified into either news or entertainment. It wasn't long until this line became blurred between these two distinctions. *Police Story* was the first police drama aired in 1952 on CBS. *Police Story* was a live, half-hour program which dramatized actual crimes depicted from files of law enforcement agencies around the nation. Between 1973–77 the more familiar *Police Story* series aired on NBC. During 1998 four made-for-television movies based on the original script of *Police Story* aired on ABC, created by Los Angeles police officer and writer Joseph Wambaugh. This police drama laid the groundwork for future reality-based police programs such as *Law & Order, Cops,* and *CSI.* (Jerin & Fields, 2005)

Our knowledge of crime news appears to emanate from various sources: the written word, television, radio, and movies. The more increase in the coverage of crime stories, such as they are, the larger the audience, and the greater the need for policy changes regarding how stories are handled in the media and which stories should be covered. There have been studies that demonstrate the more we read and watch, particularly young people, the more crime is noted. After all, crime stories draw our attention, and the media plays on our morbid curiosity.

The truthfulness of the reporting impacts the viewer's/reader's perception of crime. Yet there are victims of certain crimes who never report their stories and therefore go unnoticed by the media. When we talk about crime waves, we can turn only to recent studies, which have indicated that such waves can be attributed to the media and not to factual reporting.

> The first crusade that portrayed a crime wave was associated with the opium dens in the turn of the twentieth century. Soon after crusader Harry Anslinger used propaganda such as "Assassin of Youth" and "Reefer Madness" to validate the evils of marijuana. A report presented to the State Department by William Howard Taft in 1910 stated "the illicit sale of [cocaine] . . . and the habitual use of it temporarily raises the power of a criminal to a point where in resisting arrest there is no hesitation to murder." (Inciardi & McElrath, 2001, p. 101)

As a result of such assertions, police departments purportedly switched from the use of a .32 caliber to a .38 caliber revolver.

Inciardi and McElrath stated that "Tom Brokaw reported on *NBC News* in 1986 that crack was 'flooding America' and that crack was 'America's drug of choice.'" It was argued by Reinarman and Levine (1997) that at the time of such press releases, there were no statistics to support this allegation.

How does the media report what occurs in the criminal justice system? Much of this publicity reflects poorly on the police, the courts, and the system as a whole. While one has only to pick up a daily newspaper, or listen to the radio, or watch television news on a daily basis, one would assume that crime is rampant due to the reporting of so many stories. Action movies depict all the gore and horror of crime, adding to the perception of viewers.

This work spotlights the mass media and how it has transformed the criminal justice system into what it is today, and what that transformation has done to the system. The focus of this work—the media and its handling of the criminal justice system—will appeal to all students of criminal justice as well as those studying the arts.

The case descriptions and the commentary will fascinate readers and will set the tone for a better understanding of what we refer to as the *mediafication* of the criminal justice system.

# CHAPTER

# 2

# What About the Media?

The media continues to exert the greatest influence on the public's perception of crime. Is the presentation of criminal justice issues by the media entertainment, or is the dramatization of crime a reality check? Some researchers point out that our understanding and "wisdom" regarding criminal incidents surface from other sources as well.

> Feinberg (2002) conducted a content analysis of newspaper articles and found that increased coverage of crime produces a significant effect on the size of the police agency and policy making. Dowler (2002) found that crime-drama viewers were more likely to "favor eased restrictions on concealed guns" and "are more likely to think that being armed is advantageous" (p. 210). This does not mean that the public is blind to the influence of the media. One particular study conducted by the Center for Media and Public Affairs (1999) found "popular culture (television, movies, music, video games, etc.) was the most frequently cited source of blame for the outbreak of violence in our nation's schools" (p. 76), consuming 40 percent of the study's responses. (Jerin & Fields, 2005)

The most reliable data on the subject of crime makes it obvious that the "vast majority of people living in the United States have not been and never will be victims of crime. In fact, over 90 percent of the U.S. population has no direct experience with crime at all" (Barkan, 1997; Kappeler, Blumberg, & Potter, 1996). And "yet the public remains convinced of the imminent danger—changing their personal habits and lives to accommodate these fears and voting for politicians who promise solutions to the problem" (Potter & Kappeler, 2000, p. 2). Where then do the media get such opinions, fears, and impressions, which are unmistakably flawed?

There exists the conviction that what the media presents is mistaken and unsound. The conclusion reached by these researchers is that the "percentage of violent crimes does not match official statistics" (Jerin & Fields, 2005, p. 77). But the question to be asked is: How much of the crime that does occur is actually reported and is truthfully reported? If there are discrepancies in these "official" statistics, then are we to anticipate the "cultural products of mass media to reflect the social reality of crime" (Jerin & Fields, p. 77)?

There has been much research with regard to crime reporting and its impact on the populace (see Barak, 1994; Bennett, 2000; Cottle, 1993; Feinberg, 2002; Fox & Van Sickel, 2001; Hochstetler, 2001; Jerin & Fields, 1994, 2005; Klite, Bardwell, & Salzman, 1997; Miller, 1998; Newman, 1990; Potter & Kappeler, 1998; Sacco & Trotman, 1990; Schlesinger, Tumber, & Murdock, 1991; Sheley & Ashkins, 1981). What each one of these researchers has revealed is that "the true pictures of crime, criminals and dangerousness are out of proportion to actual crime statistics" (Jerin & Fields, 2005, p. 77).

What we do know for certain is that the reporting of crime impacts the average citizen's sensitivity to crime as well as fear of crime. For many centuries,

> the only means of disseminating knowledge from one person to another was orally. [With] new technologies there has been a creation of a maelstrom of information. The mass media can disseminate messages literally with the speed of light and sound. Publishers produce thousands of books about crime—some fictional, some true, some simply crude "potboilers." Movies [have made] crime a central theme. Producers know that movies like *Seven, Kiss the Girls, The Usual Suspects* and *Natural Born Killers* attract large audiences. Television programs also use crime and violence to attract attention. Police programs have been a staple of television programming from [the days] of *Dragnet* to *NYPD Blue*. (Potter & Kappeler, pp. 2–3)

The majority of people never have any direct familiarity with the criminal justice system. Their knowledge comes from the system as presented in the media, both verbal and written. "According to a national survey, nearly two-thirds of people get most of their views from television, contrasted to 20 percent from newspapers, 7 percent from radio, and less than 10 percent from friends, neighbors, co-workers, or personal experience" (Morin, 1997, in Jerin & Fields, p. 77). Crimes are sensationalized by the media and may or may not reflect the reality of the current situation. For example, in New York City in 2004, the rate of crime was far lower than the year before. But, if you watched television, read newspapers and magazines, or listened to the radio, you would think crime was rampant. Never a day went by without the reporting of a homicide, a drunk-driving incident, a robbery, a rape, a burglary, a case of arson, gang activity, and so on. Crime does not go away; it stays, regardless of the statistics. It is interesting, though, that "victimization data establishes that over a person's life the likelihood of victimization is very high; however, fewer than half of these cases are even reported to authorities and from the known crimes, only a very small percentage is related to a conclusion in the justice system" (Macguire et al., 1993, in Jerin & Fields, p. 77).

In a "USA Today/CNN/Gallup Poll (1993), 69 percent of the 1,000 adults polled (plus an over-sample of blacks) felt that local television news accurately reflects the amount of crime. . . . [Also] 58 percent of blacks in the sample agreed. The poll additionally found that only 25 percent of those responding believe that TV news exaggerated the amount of crime, and nine out of ten believed that crime was worse than it had been a year earlier" (Jerin & Fields, p. 77). There exists a misconception of how much crime actually occurs.

An axiom exists that proclaims "If it bleeds, it leads." This adage has become a staple of the news industry. "In 1993 the three major networks (CBS, NBC, and ABC) ran 1,632 crime stories on their evening newscasts, up from 785 the previous year and from 571 in 1991" (Potter & Kappeler, p. 3). Crime sells.

Relying on work conducted by Jerin and Fields, an early investigation of the public's understanding of crime "was an examination of how the press fabricated a 'crime wave' in 1991" (Schlesinger et al., 1991). It was "through the use of increased coverage and a call for government action [that] the public was erroneously led to believe that the crime problem was becoming much worse even though actual change was minimal" (Jerin & Fields, p. 76). It was Philip Jenkins, in *Synthetic Panics: The Symbolic Politics of Designer Drugs* (1999), who highlighted "the role of the mass media in distributing anti-drug hysteria and illustrate[d] how synthetic panics influence popular culture." The media's role has been to make possible the wave of crime. We are informed that the wave of crime that was associated with opium dens (as previously mentioned) at the beginning of the twentieth century was a result of the actions taken by the media. Harry Anslinger was a crusader who, through the use of misinformation, was able to authenticate the evils of marijuana. "A report presented to the State Department by William Howard Taft in 1910, stated 'the illicit sale of [cocaine] . . . and the habitual use of it temporarily raises the power of a criminal to a point where in resisting arrest there is no hesitation to murder' " (Inciardi, 2001, p. 101, as reported by Jerin & Fields, p. 78). Research indicates that some of these assertions forced Southern police forces to switch from the use of a .32 caliber gun to a .38 caliber revolver.

Accordingly, "Inciardi reported that Tom Brokaw reported on *NBC Nightly News* in 1986 that crack was 'flooding America' and that crack was 'America's drug of choice'" (Jerin & Fields, p. 78). Yet, there existed no statistics supporting this assertion. Other researchers found that the "*Washington Post* ran 1,565 stories about the crack crisis during the rise of the crack epidemic in 1989" (p. 78). As a result, there was an increased use of the presentation of synthetic and designer drugs being used. One had only to view shows such as *60 Minutes, 20/20, or Dateline,* all designed to be entertaining and informative, but not necessarily reflecting the true picture.

According to Potter and Kappeler,

> in addition to devoting a disproportionate amount of coverage to crime, the mass media organize coverage in a way that seriously distorts the reality of crime. First, the media provide a distorted view of how much crime there is in society. Second, media coverage of crime seriously distorts public perception of the types of crime being committed and the frequency with which violent crimes occur. The media have a preoccupation with violent crime. In the film *Die Hard II,* 264 people are killed. In *Robocop II,* another 81 victims are claimed. (p. 4)

The media covers the less common crimes as if they were common, everyday occurrences. How accurately does the media portray the criminal justice system? There exist fictitious depictions of crime waves as well as other crime-related information, all of which reflect the branches of the criminal justice system in a poor light. Polls have been taken (USA Today/CNN/Gallup Poll of 1993), which found that based on the media's presentation of the alleged facts, the courts need to deal with criminals more harshly than is being done. "Given the public's lack of personal contact with what the courts achieve, this perception of the quality of justice being dispensed is being driven by other sources" (Jerin & Fields, p. 79). Due to the many inaccuracies of the media's handling of the criminal justice system, there exist inaccuracies in the truth.

Bogus beliefs "abound in U.S. society and play a disproportionate role in the formulation of government and law enforcement policies. Despite panics about increasing crime emanating from the state and the media, the fact remains that there was no crime wave in the 1980s and 1990s; crime had been falling precipitously for two decades" (Potter & Kappeler, p. 12). In fact, it is pointed out that there existed no crack epidemic during the mid-1980s. "The crime that does exist is not predominantly violent and violent crime is not as common or debilitating as the media would lead us to believe. The media, the state, and criminal justice officials create and perpetuate crime myths" (Potter & Kappeler, p. 12).

# The Relationship
# of Crime Reporting
# to the Fear of Crime

As a society, we are fascinated by crime. According to Todd Clear, we are "a media nation" (Surette, 1998, p. ix). Crime chatter is heard everywhere. From films, newspapers, books, magazines, online articles, television, radio, to daily conversations, crime is a focal point of discussion. Which came first—fear of actual crime, or the reporting of crime that instills the fear? In an early study by Graber (1980), results indicated that "individuals who watch a large amount of television are more likely to feel a greater threat from crime, believe that crime is more prevalent than statistics indicate, and take more precautions against crime" (Dowler, 2002, p. 2). Crime as it is portrayed on television shows itself to be more dangerous, more threatening, more violent, and certainly more random than in the real world. However, there has been research that shows no direct relationship between fear of crime and crime itself.

Sources of crime are multifaceted. "The media and crime and justice must all be approached as parts of larger phenomena that have numerous interconnections and paths of influence among them" (Surette, p. 2).

"Presentation of large amounts of local crime news engenders increased fear among the larger public, while the presentation of large amounts of non-local crime news has the opposite effect by making the local viewers feel safe in comparison to other areas" (Dowler, p. 2). There is a relationship between local and national news and crime. "The effect of local news on fear of crime is stronger for residents in high crime areas and those who experience[d] victimization" (ibid.). Crime, similar to an economic recession, is practiced as both a private trouble and public issue.

Research demonstrates that those residing in high crime areas fear crime more than those living in other areas because of the way crime is reported by the media. "Another important factor is whether audience members have direct victim experience or share characteristics that make them crime vulnerable. Research indicates that media sources will be more meaningful when direct experience is lacking" (Dowler, p. 2).

We were a nation of violence long before the reporting by the media. If we were to censor the media crime would not cease to be. As pointed out by Surette, "[t]he criminal justice system acquires its legitimizing function by serving as a social arena in which the significance and value of various social behaviors are determined. It serves not only as an institution through which legal disputes are resolved but also as a mechanism through which a society's laws and system of government are legitimized" (Dowler, p. 3).

After examining research findings from the *National Opinion on Crime and Justice* (NOCJS), the fact is that "local media attention to crime was significantly related to fear of sexual assault; getting mugged, beaten up, knifed or shot; and being burglarized while at home. Fear of crime was not significantly related to fear of carjacking, being murdered or being burglarized while not at home" (Dowler, p. 3).

It is the news media, itself, that affords us a central discussion where private troubles become seized upon. Fascinatingly enough, the basis of crime news is not considered a factor in the fear of crime. It is argued that the public's dread and apprehension is intertwined with the public's pressure to find answers to the problems of crime. There are those who believe that with the over-reporting of crime, per se, there is more of a movement afoot to find solutions. "Presentations of crime news increase public pressure for more effective policing and more punitive responses to agents of crime control as negatively ineffective and incompetent which results in support for more police, more prisons, and more money for the criminal justice system" (Dowler, p. 3). The reporting of crime is a long-lasting news commodity. There is also a high level of aggression of actions asked for those who break the law. Punitive attitudes develop as a result of the reporting of crime and the viewing of crime-related shows.

> Analyses of media content demonstrate that the news provides a map of the world of criminal events that differs in many ways from one provided by official crime statistics. Variations in the volume of news about crime seem to bear little relationship to variations in the actual volume of crime between places and time. Whereas crime statistics indicate that most crime is nonviolent, media reports suggest, in the aggregate, that the opposite is true. While crime news tends to provide only sparse details about victims and offences, that which is provided is frequently at odds with the official picture. (Potter & Kappeler, 1998, p. 38)

In studying the role of the media, we must look at what Surette refers to as the *construction of reality:* ". . . people create reality—the world they believe exists—based on their individual knowledge and from knowledge gained from social interactions with other people. People then act in accordance with their constructed view of reality" (p. 5). "Knowledge is by necessity conditioned by the structure of society and the social conditions that at least partly determine what constitutes knowledge for a particular group" (p. 6). Accepting this factor we can understand why there is so much interest in the role of the mass media on American culture. There are many ways of gaining knowledge. One can gain such knowledge from one's peers, families, friends, from personal experiences, from social groups and from institutions such as schools and governmental agencies.

> Since the sources of knowledge people use to socially construct reality vary in importance, the degree of media contribution to the individual's construction of reality is a function of one's direct experience with various phenomena and consequent dependence on the media for information. The symbolic reality knowledge you obtain from significant others is usually more influential that what you receive from social institutions or the mass media. In modern, advanced, industrialized societies with strong popular cultures, the mass media have emerged as a main engine in the social construction of reality process. (Surette, p. 7)

In the United States, the media is a major organization from which we derive our information. We appear to depend a great deal on the social reality created by the media. "In their operational routines, the media impose constraints on the images that are socially available while presenting social problems within familiar frames and cultural terms" (p. 7). It is not that we accept the media at face value, but rather that it is a means "for various constructions of crime, law, and justice to compete for public acceptance" (p. 7).

The conclusion to be reached is that media does, in fact, dictate how shared knowledge is distributed, and its effect becomes fourfold, according to Surette:

- We record and analyze history in terms of what the media define as significant.
- People with potential historical importance must rely on media exposure to ensure their place in history.
- Media reports become an essential determination of what is held to be significant as media influence becomes ever more widely known and accepted.
- Institutions find they must present their own message and images within the accepted respectability and familiarity of media-determined formats. (pp. 7–8).

There are organizational constraints with regard to the dissemination of information, as evidenced in the effectiveness of the police.


## HOW EFFECTIVE ARE THE POLICE?

How effective is law enforcement? Most studies indicate that the media distorts the relationship between crime control and legal factors. Often, the shows that depict crime indicate that the police are the heroes, the ones who are the crime fighters and protectors of the law. Most crime shows—*Law & Order* and *NYPD Blue,* to name a couple— have the crime solved at the end of the hour and show police to be more effective than they are in real-life situations. "The favorable view of policing is partly a consequence of the police's public relations strategy. Reporting of proactive police activity creates an image of the police as effective and efficient investigators of crime. Accordingly, a positive police portrayal reinforces traditional approaches to law and order that involves increased police presence, harsher penalties and increasing police power" (Dowler, p. 3).

There apparently exists a keen relationship between the media and the police. "The media needs the police to provide them with quick, reliable sources of crime information, while the police have a vested interest in maintaining a positive public image. . . . [However, there are claims] that docu-dramas and news tabloid programs represent the police as heroes that fight evil, yet print and broadcast news personify the police as ineffective and incompetent" (Dowler, p. 3). There are those who contend that the public evaluates the work of the police more favorably than that of the courts and correction. Accordingly, "the media provides little information to judge police and . . . the news media focus on negative criticism rather than positive or successful crime prevention efforts. . . . Most media crime is punished, but policemen are rarely the heroes" (p. 3).

What is the relationship between media consumption and the fear of crime? What is the relationship between media consumption and punitive attitudes? And what is the relationship between media consumption and public ratings of police effectiveness? Crime news has an elastic character inasmuch as on any one day, more likely in metropolitan areas than in suburban or rural areas, there is an endless supply of crimes, any one of which could very well develop into the focus of media attention. Depending on what is happening in the world, the amount, the kinds of crime stories written, and the placement of such stories varies.

Studies appear to indicate that crime-show viewing is related to the fear of crime. Studies also hold that the worse the neighborhood, the higher the fear of crime. The feeling is that

> the strongest indicator of punitive attitudes is race, followed by education, income, fear of crime, and marital status. African-American respondents are more likely to hold non-punitive attitudes. . . . The result of inequalities of the justice system. . . . Compared to whites, African-Americans are more likely to receive harsher punishments (such as the death penalty)[1] and African Americans are disproportionately over-represented in prisons.[2] Some African Americans may feel threatened by a punitive justice model or feel that a punitive justice model reinforces discrimination and persecution of African Americans. (Dowler, p. 10)

Those who live in high crime areas and view these shows have a high fear of crime, females in particular. What is interesting is that those individuals who are college graduates have more fear of crime, yet being the most highly educated, one would assume (and apparently wrongly) that they would understand about the media and not be unduly influenced.

> However, college educated [individuals] may feel that they have more to "lose" if they are victimized. . . . Regular viewers of crime drama are

---

[1]However, the majority of defendants on death row are white.
[2]This is true.

more likely to fear crime [as] television portrayal of crime and justice is largely sensational, violent and fear producing. Viewers may receive a "distorted" image of the typical crime or criminal which may produce fear or anxiety about criminal activity. Compared to respondents with average incomes of $30K to $60K, lower income respondents are more likely to fear crime. (Dowler, p. 10)

Again, those who are educated recognize the inequalities of the criminal justice system and believe that rehabilitation or reintegration programs offer better answers than imprisonment. "Compared to average income respondents, low-income respondents ($15,000 to $30,000) are more likely to hold punitive attitudes toward crime and justice. This is in contrast to the lowest income [individuals] ($15,000 or less) . . . who feel that they have more to 'lose' by victimization" (Dowler, p. 10). All of this is because of the influence of the media.

How effective are the police as depicted by the media? There are mixed signals. There appears to be little concurrence on the role that is portrayed by the police in drama shows as compared to real life. Results of all studies indicate that age is a prime factor, as well as problems within viewers' neighborhoods. A fear of crime comes from the way crime is portrayed by the media. Those who fear crime and see crime have much to fear.

However, there is the feeling that African Americans view the police in a hostile manner and that whites are treated better than African-Americans, both in reality and by the media.

Research indicates that there is a significant association between being black and being harassed by police. Other factors may include an increased awareness of police corruption, racism, brutality and racial profiling. A number of significant "social" events occurred during the 1990s [to make this view even more acceptable]. For example, the beating of Rodney King and the racist remarks of Mark Fuhrman elevated racism and police brutality into a national issue [very much viewed by the populace]. . . . We have seen racial profiling or "driving while black" emerge as an important social issue. (Dowler, p. 11)

Regular viewers of crime stories fear crime. "There are numerous types of crime shows that may focus on different aspects of the criminal justice system. . . . Crime shows may focus on police, courts, private investigators, defense lawyers and sometimes even the criminal. [And] it would be naïve to suggest that respondents are not affected by a number of sources; for example respondents who receive their primary crime news from newspapers may also be affected by presentations of crime from other sources such as films, television and/or personal experience" (Dowler, pp. 11–12).

## SUMMING UP

The fear of crime is a natural reaction to violence, brutality, and the injustice that is broadcast daily. It is true that there is an overemphasis on crime by the media.

> There is an overemphasis on crimes of violence and offenders are often portrayed in stereotypical ways. For example, murder and robbery dominate [the news] while property crimes are rarely presented. Offenders are often viewed as psychopaths that prey on weak and vulnerable victims. [And] in other cases, offenders are portrayed as businessmen or professionals that are shrewd, ruthless and violent. Television crime is exciting and a rewarding endeavor, whereas victims are passive, helpless and vulnerable. (Dowler, p. 12)

Most viewers have little or no understanding of the workings of the criminal justice system. The system itself is portrayed by the media as ineffective, with the exceptions of some "heroes."

> Crime shows rarely focus on mitigating issues of criminal behavior and are unlikely to portray offenders in a sympathetic or even realistic fashion. On television, crime is freely chosen and based on individual problems of the offender. Analysis of crime dramas reveal that greed, revenge and mental illness are the basic motivations for crime and offenders are often portrayed as "different" from the general population. . . . Viewers . . . believe that all offenders are "monsters" to be feared. (Dowler, p. 12)

What the results do indicate is not that the perception of police effectiveness is somehow interconnected with the consumption of the media. The fact is that African Americans who view and subsequently report criminal acts feel that the police do not respond properly. The fact that the media reports these crimes that transpire in high-crime areas is shown to be a cause and effect of attitudes within these areas. If African Americans give poor ratings to police effectiveness, it is because of such reporting. One could conclude that the media plays a role in "influencing" the population.

> Abstract danger legitimizes public surveillance and regimented personal action by forging the spectacle between the media, the audience, and comprehensive social control. The real power to control crime pales in comparison to the illusion of control and the universalized desire to control the "evil" that is inscribed in even the most insipid media accounts of crime. The perpetrator walk—marching the accused person in handcuffs before a crew of reporters and cameras—feeds the desire for justice. The criminal is reduced to the glare of publicity, caught by the system of control that protects all of us. It is a compelling

drama for the media to project to an audience eager to believe that the system of control works. The spectacle of reality produced by mass-media images reduces life, justice and the real crime that exist to something less than the abstraction. (Potter & Kappeler, p. 339)

Perhaps part of the problem is that unlike reporters, law enforcement officers are bound by rules and regulations that can either aid or hinder an investigation. While both reporters and police officers might set out with the same goal in mind, such as determining guilt or innocence, a reporter has few restrictions and can angle a story to presume guilt or innocence with little or no ramifications. Understanding this difference and the subtleties can often determine how a story will be covered, and consequently how the public perceives crime. Shelly Feuer Domash had the opportunity to spend six months as a recruit in the Nassau County, New York, police academy writing a series of articles for the *New York Times* on becoming a police officer. It enabled her to witness a different side of the "blue wall." As a result, her perspective changed and her articles became more in depth and consistently different from the coverage of other reporters, without favoring any one side.

We know for a fact that the media consumes a lot of our attention and unduly influences us, particularly when we lack knowledge. Regular viewing of crime shows affects our attitude and fear of crime. The world of law enforcement is complicated at best, and perhaps a better understanding and more communication is needed between reporters and police.

# Crimes and Reactions

It was Walter Cronkite who, upon retiring from being the anchor person on CBS, stated that his reporting of nightly news was "rewarding" but not entirely "satisfactory." Time limitations prevented him from doing the in-depth reporting necessary. You cannot cover all the news in seventeen minutes, the allotted time without commercial interruptions, according to Cronkite. He found that many stories, in particular those reported on the Web, are played too fast and too loose. Factually, the story was not reported as it should be, or as it was. Cronkite said, "I am dumbfounded that there hasn't been a crackdown with the libel and slander laws on some of these would-be writers and reporters on the Internet. I expect that to develop in the fairly near future" (*New York Times*, 2004, p. A12).

## CRIME STORIES THAT BRING A SMILE

There are some stories that give you a good laugh, stories that are real, but somewhat funny.[1]

**South Carolina**   A man walked into a local police station, dropped a bag of cocaine on the counter, informed the desk sergeant that it was substandard cut, and asked that the person who sold it to him be arrested immediately.

---

[1]*Source:* From the Web site Clumsy Crooks—Funny Real-Life Crime Stories and Pictures About Dumb Criminals, www.clumsycrooks.com. Retrieved February 15, 2004.

**Case Closed**   After representing himself in court and twice winning acquittals on charges of writing worthless checks and assault, Reinero Torres, Jr., of Sebring, Florida, lost a third case. He was convicted of theft for having stolen law books from the courthouse library to prepare his defense for the first two cases.

**Not the Sharpest Knife in the Drawer**   In Modesto, California, Steven Richard King was arrested for trying to hold up a Bank of America branch without a weapon. King used a thumb and a finger to simulate a gun, but unfortunately, he failed to keep his hand in his pocket.

**Set Up**   A company called "Guns for Hire" stages gunfights for Western movies, etc. One day, they received a call from a 47-year-old woman, who wanted to have her husband killed. She got 4½ years in jail.

**Too Many Pennies**   David Posman, 33, was arrested in Providence, Rhode Island, after knocking out an armored car driver and stealing four bags of money. Each bag contained $80. However, the bags weighed thirty pounds each since they all contained PENNIES. The hefty bags slowed the fleeing Posman to a sluggish stagger. Police easily ran down and arrested the suspect.

**Run Over**   An English bank robber planned the perfect heist. Every detail was perfectly orchestrated: the ideal robbery time; the type of gun to use; a place to hide the loot; a getaway route and car; and even a reliable accomplice. After robbing the bank, the man left with the money in a bag over his left shoulder. As he approached the spot of the getaway car, his accomplice promptly ran over him.

**One Dumb Crook**   A fellow robbed a supermarket of about $5000. The local newspaper ran the story, but with the amount given as $7000. The thief called the newspaper to complain abut the inaccuracy and to suggest that maybe the store manager ripped off the extra $2000 and was unjustly blaming the thief. The people at the newspaper kept him busy on the phone giving his version of the story while the police traced the call to a phone booth and arrived to arrest him while he was still talking to the newspaper!

**Thanks for the "Tip"**   A man broke into a jewelry store in the middle of the night. Once inside he broke the glass case to extract the jewelry—so excited and anxious to get his hands on the diamonds in the case he did not notice that when he broke the glass with his hand, he cut the tip end of his finger off. When police did arrive, they merely fished the top portion of the finger out, printed it, and ran a match program. The man was arrested within a few hours of his crime.

# 5

# The Salem Witchcraft Trials

According to Nash (1982), "seventeenth-century writing is permeated with the idea of the wild country as the environment of evil. The New World wilderness was linked with a host of monsters, witches and similar supernatural beings" (p. 29). Evil was seen looming in the wilderness and uncontrollable.

The modern criminal justice system is viewed as a means to "tame the naturally wild instincts of human beings" (Wilson, 2002, p. 24). Our modern criminal justice system views nature as something to be controlled so that we can be considered safe. But the reporting of the Salem witch trials stated that sin was viewed as something inevitable on the part of the convict. At that time in history, "Puritans were intensely frightened by two kinds of wilderness—that in the forests surrounding them at the edges of their carefully cultivated fields and neat towns, and that which was within human nature, especially female human nature. Both kinds of wilderness were evil precisely because they were wild. Under the Puritan mission there was both "an inner battle over that 'desolate and outgrowne wilderness of human nature' and on the New England frontier it also meant conquering wild nature" (Wilson, p. 25). The focus of the criminal justice system was on women, as it was their relationship to nature that was considered wrong.

Women who would be considered modern in today's world were deemed a threat then. "Human reproduction was a significant concern of the Puritan witch hunters, who blamed female witches for abortions (both spontaneous and induced), 'monstrous births,' and

23

untimely deaths from disease in young children. Exertion of male control over human reproduction is still a vital concern" (Wilson, p. 26) in today's world. So if the media focused on the role of women in the seventeenth century with regard to issues such as abortion, imagine what would have been reported in today's world. Abortion issues, partial-birth abortions, embryo stem cell research, protection of bodily integrity, privacy issues that pertain to a woman and her body— these are the same issues talked about then, but in a different light and reported differently than today.

## THE SALEM WITCH TRIALS OF 1692

Follow the chronology of the events that preceded the execution of the "witches as accused":

### January 20

Nine-year-old Elizabeth Parris and eleven-year-old Abigail Williams began to exhibit strange behavior, such as blasphemous screaming, convulsive seizures, trancelike states, and mysterious spells. Within a short time, several other Salem girls began to demonstrate similar behaviors.

### Mid-February

Unable to determine any physical cause for the symptoms and dreadful behavior, physicians concluded that the girls were under the influence of Satan.

### Late February

Prayer services and community fasting were conducted by Reverend Samuel Parris in hopes of relieving the evil forces that plagued them. In an effort to expose the "witches," John Indian baked a witch cake made with rye meal and the afflicted girls' urine. This counter-magic was meant to reveal the identities of the "witches" to the afflicted girls.

Pressured to identify the source of their affliction, the girls named three women, including Tituba, Parris' Carib Indian slave, as witches. On February 29, warrants were issued for the arrests of Tituba, Sarah Good, and Sarah Osborne.

Although Osborne and Good maintained their innocence, Tituba confessed seeing the devil who appeared to her "sometimes like a hog and sometimes like a great dog." What's more, Tituba testified that there was a conspiracy of witches at work in Salem.

## March 1

Magistrates John Hathorne and Jonathan Corwin examined Tituba, Sarah Good, and Sarah Osborne in the meeting house in Salem Village. Tituba confessed to practicing witchcraft.

Over the next weeks, other townspeople came forward and testified that they, too, had been harmed by or had seen strange apparitions of some of the community members. As the witch hunt continued, accusations were made against many different people.

Frequently denounced were women whose behavior or economic circumstances were somehow disturbing to the social order and conventions of the time. Some of the accused had previous records of criminal activity, including witchcraft, but others were faithful churchgoers and people of high standing in the community.

## March 12

Martha Corey was accused of witchcraft.

## March 19

Rebecca Nurse was denounced as a witch.

## March 21

Martha Corey was examined before magistrates Hathorne and Corwin.

## March 28

Elizabeth Proctor was denounced as a witch.

## April 3

Sarah Cloyce, Rebecca Nurse's sister, was accused of witchcraft.

## April 11

Elizabeth Proctor and Sarah Cloyce were examined before Hathorne, Corwin, Deputy Governor Thomas Danforth, and Captain Samuel Sewall. During this examination, John Proctor was also accused and imprisoned.

**April 19**

Abigail Hobbs, Bridget Bishop, Giles Corey, and Mary Warren were examined. Only Abigail Hobbs confessed.

William Hobbs: "I can deny it to my dying day."

**April 22**

Nehemiah Abbott, William and Deliverance Hobbs, Edward and Sarah Bishop, Mary Easty, Mary Black, Sarah Wildes, and Mary English were examined before Hathorne and Corwin. Only Nehemiah Abbott was cleared of the charges.

**May 2**

Sarah Morey, Lydia Dustin, Susannah Martin, and Dorcas Hoar were examined by Hathorne and Corwin.

Dorcas Hoar: "I will speak the truth as long as I live."

**May 4**

George Burroughs was arrested in Wells, Maine.

**May 9**

Burroughs was examined by Hathorne, Corwin, Sewall, and William Stoughton. One of the afflicted girls, Sarah Churchill, was also examined.

**May 10**

George Jacobs, Sr., and his granddaughter, Margaret, were examined before Hathorne and Corwin. Margaret confessed and testified that her grandfather and George Burroughs were both witches.

Sarah Osborne died in prison in Boston.

Margaret Jacobs: "They told me if I would not confess I should be put down into the dungeon and would be hanged, but if I would confess I would save my life."

**May 14**

Increase Mather returned from England, bringing with him a new Charter and the new governor, Sir William Phips.

## May 27

Governor Phips set up a special Court of Oyer and Terminer comprised of seven judges to try the withcraft cases. Appointed were Lieutenant Governor William Stoughton, Nathaniel Saltonstall, Bartholomew Gedney, Peter Sergeant, Samuel Sewall, Wait Still Winthrop, John Richards, John Hathorne, and Jonathan Corwin.

These magistrates based their judgments and evaluations on various kinds of intangible evidence, including direct confessions, supernatural attributes (such as "witchmarks"), and reactions of the afflicted girls. Spectral evidence, based on the assumption that the Devil could assume the "specter" of an innocent person, was relied upon despite its controversial nature.

## May 31

Martha Carrier, John Alden, Wilmott Redd, Elizabeth Howe, and Phillip English were examined before Hathorne, Corwin, and Gedney.

## June 2

Initial session of the Court of Oyer and Terminer. Bridget Bishop was the first to be pronounced guilty and condemned to death.

## Early June

Soon after Bridget Bishop's trial, Nathaniel Saltonstall resigned from the court, dissatisfied with its proceedings.

## June 10

Bridget Bishop was hanged in Salem, the first official execution of the Salem witch trials.

Bridget Bishop: "I am no witch, I am innocent. I know nothing of it."

Following her death, accusations of witchcraft escalated, but the trials were not unopposed. Several townspeople signed petitions on behalf of accused people they believed to be innocent.

## June 29–30

Rebecca Nurse, Susannah Martin, Sarah Wildes, Sarah Good, and Elizabeth Howe were tried for witchcraft and condemned.

Rebecca Nurse: "Oh Lord, help me! It is false. I am clear. For my life now lies in your hands."

## Mid-July

In an effort to expose the witches afflicting his life, Joseph Ballard of nearby Andover enlisted the aid of the accusing girls of Salem. This action marked the beginning of the Andover witch hunt.

## July 19

Rebecca Nurse, Susannah Martin, Elizabeth Howe, Sarah Good, and Sarah Wildes were executed.

Elizabeth Howe: "If it was the last moment I was to live, God knows I am innocent."

Susannah Martin: "I have no hand in witchcraft."

## August 2–6

George Jacobs, Sr., Martha Carrier, George Burroughs, John and Elizabeth Proctor, and John Willard were tried for witchcraft and condemned.

Martha Carrier: "I am wronged. It is a shameful thing that you should mind these folks that are not of their wits."

## August 19

George Jacobs, Sr., Martha Carrier, George Burroughs, John Proctor, and John Willard were hanged on Gallows Hill.

George Jacobs: "Because I am falsely accused. I never did it."

## September 9

Martha Corey, Mary Easty, Alice Parker, Ann Pudeator, Dorcas Hoar, and Mary Bradbury were tried and condemned.

Mary Bradbury: "I do plead not guilty. I am wholly innocent of such wickedness."

## September 17

Margaret Scott, Wilmott Redd, Samuel Wardwell, Mary Parker, Abigail Faulkner, Rebecca Eamers, Mary Lacy, Ann Foster, and Abigail Hobbs were tried and condemned.

## September 19

Giles Corey was pressed to death for refusing a trial.

**September 21**

Dorcas Hoar was the first of those pleading innocent to confess. Her execution was delayed.

**September 22**

Martha Corey, Margaret Scott, Mary Easty, Alice Parker, Ann Pudeator, Wilmott Redd, Samuel Wardwell, and Mary Parker were hanged.

**October 8**

After twenty people had been executed in the Salem Witch Hunt, Thomas Brattle wrote a letter criticizing the witchcraft trials. This letter had a great impact on Governor Phips, who ordered that reliance on spectral and intangible evidence would no longer be allowed in trials.

**October 29**

Governor Phips dissolved the Court of Oyer and Terminer.

**November 25**

The General Court of the colony created the Superior Court to try the remaining witchcraft cases, which took place in May 1693. This time no one was convicted.

Mary Easty: "If it be possible no more innocent blood be shed. . . . I am clear of this sin."

And in the words of Nanci Koser Wilson (2002), "perhaps twenty-first century Americans have no more need than did our seventeenth-century ancestors to punish wild women for its immediate effect. Perhaps, now as then, the critical effect of their criminal justice process is a boundary maintenance of women, bringing their fertility under control, ordering it into a new hierarchical Great Chain of (patriarchal) Being" (p. 28).

## DISCUSSION QUESTIONS

1. Can an argument be made that what was really at the heart of the witches' crimes in Salem Village was a rebellion against the hierarchical order of society?

2. What are some contemporary examples of man's attempt to maintain control over woman's nature?

3. Contemporary Americans view witchcraft as an imaginary offense, so this episode has been viewed by most scholars as an aberration, atypical of American criminal justice. In today's world, how would the media have reported the Salem trials and the execution of "witches"?

4. Do the media see women as still being possessed? Would it be worth reporting?

5. Write a news report using the technology of today to demonstrate how these cases would be shown today.

# The Scopes Monkey Trial, 1925

Using history as an example, we review certain noteworthy cases of years gone by and see how the media influenced the populace in their handling and reporting of these cases. The headlines in 1925 stated that the Scopes Monkey Trial had rationalists challenging a Tennessee law that forbade the teaching of the theory of evolution. It was reported as "a 1925 Media Circus," and this was without the use of television or radio, but rather the blitz of the newspapers and their portrayal of what went on in the courts.

The reports stated that there was a cast of characters: Clarence Darrow was the "famed and brilliant lawyer specializing in defending underdogs, who volunteered for the cast to help combat fundamentalist ignorance." The other main actor was William Jennings Bryan, "known as the 'The Great Commoner,' a tent-revivalist three-time presidential candidate and former Secretary of State to Woodrow Wilson. His checkered political career over, he switched to the evangelism business. He said: 'I am more interested in the rock of ages than in the age of rocks.'" And then there was John T. Scopes, a twenty-four-year-old teacher of science as well as a football coach who dared to teach about evolution. The headlines during this time were as follows:

CRANKS AND FREAKS FLOCK TO DAYTON

*Strange Creeds and Theories Are Preached and Sung Within Shadow of the Court House*

## TWO APES AND "LINK" ARRIVE AT DAYTON

*Wrath of Town Placated When It Is Said That They May Be Used to Disprove Evolution. Bryan Visits Chimpanzee*

## DARROW SCORES IGNORANCE AND BIGOTRY, SEEKING TO QUASH SCOPES INDICTMENT: STATE ARGUES FOR ITS POLICE POWER

Under the headlines "STORMY SCENES IN THE TRIAL OF SCOPES, AS DARROW MOVES TO BAR ALL PRAYERS: 'LEAK' DELAYS INDICTMENT DECISION," the story read as follows:

> The world's attention was riveted on Dayton, Tennessee, during July, 1925. At issue was the constitutionality of the "Butler Law," which prohibited the teaching of evolution in the classroom. Oklahoma, Florida, Mississippi, North Carolina already had such laws. The ACLU hoped to use the Scopes case to test (and defeat) Fundamentalist meddling in politics. Judge John Raulston began the trial by reading the first 27 verses of Genesis.

The headlines read: "DARROW SCORES IGNORANCE AND BIGOTRY SEEKING TO QUASH SCOPES INDICTMENT; STATE ARGUES FOR ITS POLICE POWER." The story read as follows:

> Darrow's defense plan was to present a series of scientists and experts, but the prosecution was not about to allow Darrow to use the courtroom and the national stage to spread evolutionist heresies. They said that since the theory of evolution violated the story of creation as told in the Bible, anything the experts might say about birds and bugs would be immaterial, irrelevant, and incompetent. Judge Raulston refused to rule against the admissibility of such evidence until he had heard some of it. The jury was (once again) banished, and Dr. Maynard Metcalf, zoologist from Johns Hopkins University, took the stand. He outlined the theory of evolution, and anthropologies, and sketched briefly the development of man from primate.
>
> The packed, hot courtroom went nuts. Attorney General Steward attacked Darrow, and said that with his mind and manners he could have done great work in the service of God, and yet he had "strayed so far from the natural goal" and aligned himself with "that which strikes its fangs at the very bosom of Christianity."
>
> Hearty "Amens" from the crowd filled the air.—Darrow wheeled and glared daggers at them.

With the jury still out of the room, Bryan stood and a hush fell over the spectators. He would allow no more of this "pseudoscientific evidence to be interjected into the trial." He got "Amens," laughter and applause from the crowd with several flippant jokes: he "could quote the number of animal breeds in round numbers, but he didn't think animals bred in round numbers." The room was filled with shouted agreement when he lamented satirically "that the evolutionists wouldn't let us descend from American monkeys, only from European monkeys."

He then launched into a long sermon about the immutability of revealed religion, drawing "Amens" and increasingly thunderous applause from the audience, climaxing in a plea for Fundamentalist taxpayers' rights. The Judge called a recess.

In the morning, the Judge ruled to exclude the experts and their testimony. He based his ruling on the claim that neither religion nor evolution was on trial, that Scopes was on trial for violating a specific Tennessee law.

Darrow, after an exchange with the Judge, was charged with contempt of court, and another day passed. The next morning, Judge Raulston moved the trial onto the Courthouse lawn because of the throngs inside, with all their clapping in the 100+ degree heat, were weakening the floor and it was in danger of collapsing. On the lawn, on Sunday meeting platforms, Court was held in front of five thousand spectators.

Darrow, as a last recourse, chose his old stratagem of putting the prosecution on the defense and heightened the already rapt attention of the world by putting Bryan on the stand. If he couldn't use scientists to prove evolution, he would disprove Bryan and the Bible. It turned the tide of the trial, and of public sentiment.

Bryan faced his inquisitor.

"You have given considerable study to the Bible, haven't you, Mr. Bryan?"

"Yes I have, I have studied the Bible for about fifty years."

"Do you claim that everything in the Bible should be literally interpreted?"

"I believe that everything in the Bible should be accepted as it is given there."

"Do you believe Joshua made the sun stand still?"

"I believe what the Bible says."

"I suppose you mean that the earth stood still?"

"I don't know. I am talking about the Bible now. I accept the Bible absolutely."

More questions show that Bryan understands the workings of the solar system, then Darrow asks:

(Darrow)   You believe the story of the flood to be a literal
           interpretation?

*(Bryan)*    Yes sir.

*(Darrow)*    When was that flood?

*(Bryan)*    I would not attempt to fix the day.

*(Darrow)*    But what do you think the Bible itself says? Don't you know how it was arrived at?

*(Bryan)*    I never made a calculation.

*(Darrow)*    What do you think?

*(Bryan)*    I do not think about things I don't think about.

*(Darrow)*    Do you think about the things you do think about?

*(Bryan)*    Well sometimes.

And so it is reported. It was reported in the papers that the crowd was now laughing at Bryan and not Darrow. Persistent questioning by Darrow of Bryan proved Bryan to be what was reported as a near imbecile.

Headlines were made in Europe as well: "Europe Is Amazed by the SCOPES Case." On July 11, 1925, the Rev. Frank Ballard, a Christian Evidence lecturer, wrote:

> The assumptions of fundamentalism are so preposterous . . . it is pitifully manifest that both the science and theology of many of those posing as authorities are half a century behind the times. The notion of the Judge's charge to the Grand Jury beginning with the reading of the First Chapter of Genesis as an account of creation which Tennessee teachers must adopt savors of the sixteenth century rather than the twentieth century.

In Paris on July 13, 1925, headlines read "French Satirize the Case." Although there was no discussion of the issues involved, the French press followed closely the developments in the Dayton case and occasionally burst out into cynical observations on the subject.

The *Paris Soir*, describing the case as one that would decide whether "a monkey or Adam was the grandfather of Uncle Sam," wrote:

> On this side of the ocean it is difficult to understand the susceptibility of American citizens on the subject and precisely why they should so stubbornly cling to the biblical version. It is said in Genesis the first man came from mud and mud is not anything very clean. In any case, if the Darwinian hypothesis should irritate anyone, it should be the monkey. The monkey is an innocent animal—a vegetarian by birth. He has never placed God on a cross, knows nothing of the art of war, does not practice the lynch law and never dreams of assassinating his fellow

beings. The day when science definitely recognizes him as the father of the human race the monkey will have no occasion to be proud of his descendants. That is why it must be concluded that the American Association which is prosecuting the teacher of evolution can be no other than the Society for Prevention of Cruelty to Animals.

The headlines once again read, "Crowds Jam Court to See Champions." On July 15, 1925, the headlines stated that "Bryan and Darrow Exchange Gifts of Carved Monkeys."

This was the beginning of the twentieth century. The furor that this case caused, the arguments that ensued, were attributed to most of what was reported by the news media.

In an Epilogue prepared by the media:

> Only five days after the trial ended, Bryan lay down for a Sunday afternoon nap and never woke up. His lifelong diabetes and gluttonous eating habits had finally taken their toll. The trial itself melted into insignificance when more than a year later, on January 14, 1927, the State Supreme Court in Nashville handed down a decision which reversed the earlier one. However, the court's decision stemmed from the very point Darrow sought to avoid—a technicality. By Tennessee state law, the jury, not the judge, must set the fine if is above $50. The Butler Law, then, stood untested. The image of Fundamentalism, however, was irrevocably tarnished. They had proven themselves to be the "yokels, bigots, and rubes," as the press had called them.
>
> To this day, there exist those people who deny that all life is connected. It is their belief that humans are part of the equation. There is inconsistency among Fundamentalists. How life was created is still left for debate among many, but the media had played a large part in influencing others. (Stone, 1941; Mencken, 1926)

As a postscript, many of the residents of Tennessee at the time were embarrassed by the whole proceeding. They felt the necessity of getting rid of the stereotype of the ignorant Southerner that had plagued them for many years. The newspapers at the time throughout both the state and the country attacked the whole town. Initially, they indicated that it was just a publicity stunt, but that did not stop the throngs of reporters from going to Dayton. H. L. Mencken of the *Baltimore Sun* wrote disrespectfully about the trial proceedings, while the *Sun* itself offered to pay the fine of Scopes if he were to be found guilty.

This brings to mind the day that the decision was to be announced regarding O.J. Simpson. The jury had come in the day before with their decision, but the decision was not to be announced until the following day for fear of riots. At one college campus, minority students were urged to come to the student cafeteria and sit front of the television monitors that were set up. The reporters were to be there to take pictures of the students as they heard the decision. Ideally, the students would be cheering. Faculty were encouraged to do likewise, but most stayed in their offices, not wishing to be so manipulated by the media. Manipulation is a favorite tool of the media.

The media reported on Bryan and how he believed that "ape-ism" was an unparalleled risk to the purity of all mankind. Darrow was written about as being an agnostic, an atheist. The scene around the courthouse was described as being very unique and was referred to as "Monkeyville."

Can we imagine what the scene would have been had there been television cameras and Court TV around?

## DISCUSSION QUESTIONS

1. How do you think the media would have reported the story of the Scopes trial if it occurred today?
2. Think of the famous attorneys of today. How would they have handled the media regarding evolution?
3. Did the media convince the citizens that the decision was right or wrong?

# 7

# The Menendez Brothers, 1989

Children who kill their parents is the kind of story that the media loves, and the saga of the Menendez brothers was a perfect fit. It was also notable in that it was a case in which the court was forced to acknowledge the influence of the media on the outcome of a trial. After a deadlocked jury, the judge banned cameras from a second trial. And certainly, if the media's influence on a trial was documented in this case, it has happened many times before.

Their story is what books are written about. The daily news media loves it, and the public can't seem to get enough of it. The facts become a drama, and that drama takes on a life of its own.

> A man and a woman are found slaughtered in their luxurious Beverly Hills home. A crime scene soaked in blood. Wealthy, attractive, clean-cut defendants with a seemingly clear motive for the murders. A riveting, controversial and protracted televised trial. And a jury decision that stunned many Americans, who had thought that the only possible outcome of the trial was a guilty verdict. (Gleick, 1995)

With all of that, what more could the media want to sell papers or attract viewers?

The story began on the evening of August 20, 1989, in Beverly Hills, California. It was a quiet night inside the $4 million, twenty-three-room mansion on Elm Drive. Jose and Kitty Menendez were watching television. Their two sons, Lyle, twenty-one, and Erik, eighteen, had gone out for the evening. The gates to the home were open and the security system was off. Two men entered the home. A later reenactment of the crime by the police and medical examiner would reveal that two shots were fired at Jose, hitting his arms. Then the intruders walked behind him and shot him in his head. The shots woke up Kitty, who began to run. She was hit in the leg and arm. She struggled to stand up, but was shot again numerous times. Despite bleeding heavily, she again tried to escape. The killers were out of ammunition. They ran to the car, reloaded, and placed the shotgun against Kitty's cheek. She was shot ten times. Her skull was shattered.

The killers carefully gathered all the shell casings and fled the blood-soaked scene. This would be a difficult case to solve, but one that initially did not attract much national media attention. Police delved into the lives of the victims in an attempt to find the killers.

A profile of Jose revealed him to be an unpopular, difficult man, who had earned a reputation of making it difficult for his subordinates. He allegedly had a series of mistresses as well. According to the Court TV Web site, when his sons were young, Jose had rules for everything, what the children were to eat, whom they could spend time with, and what they read and thought about.

> The pressures of meeting Jose's demands appeared early on Lyle and Erik. Both brothers developed stutters, stomach pains and had a habit of grinding their teeth. Both brothers also developed nasty tempers. At the age of 14, Lyle still wet his bed and played with stuffed animals. (Pergament, 2003)

The brothers had a series of problems. Lyle was accused of plagiarism while at Princeton and was eventually put on disciplinary probation; both brothers had been accused of breaking into homes in Calabasas, California, in 1988.

They also stood to inherit a great deal of money in the event of their parents' deaths. Four days after their parents were killed, the boys went on a spending spree. They bought new cars, designer clothing, and expensive jewelry. They found out that they were going to inherit $2 million each, which records indicate was less than they had expected.

Since Jose was not a popular man, and in fact had many enemies, the police were having a difficult time solving the double homicide. The police were becoming suspicious of the two brothers. Within a year they had spent almost a million dollars. Still, there was not a great deal of national publicity about the murders. Most people who were not in the immediate area were not affected, assuming it had something to do with the couple, since nothing was taken from the home.

The savagery of the crime and stature of the victims guaranteed head-lines from the start. . . . But the story didn't make the cover of *People Magazine* until seven months later, when the suspects were finally arrested. They turned out to be not a couple of mob gunmen, as first thought, but the Menendezes' swaggering sons: Lyle, 22, who left Princeton after being caught cheating, and Erik, 19, a writer of poems and screenplays who tried unsuccessfully to make it as a pro tennis player. (Gibbs, 1990)

Eventually, Erik told his therapist he had killed his parents. He said he and his brother were watching the *Billionaire Boys Club* mini-series, and they talked about how they thought their father was planning to disinherit them. He related how they committed the crime and what they did with the gun afterwards. When Lyle heard about the confession, he was furious and told the therapist he would kill him if he revealed their secret.

The therapist, Jerome Oziel, kept their secret, until his alleged lover, Judalon Smyth, who knew about the confession, went to the police. Police obtained a search warrant and got copies of the therapist's notes and tapes of the sessions. Gibbs wrote,

For months after the stunning arrest, stories circulated about the relationship between Oziel and the police informant. She turns out to be Judalon Smyth, his alleged one-time lover and sometime patient, who published a newsletter for doll collectors and produced audio cassettes like *Insights into the Sensuality and Sexuality of the Aquarius Woman.* Her steamy story was laid out this month in *Vanity Fair* by reporter Dominick Dunne; in the article she explains that Oziel hypnotized her over the phone into falling in love with him. Two weeks ago, she filed a lawsuit charging Oziel drugged and raped her and later forced her to eaves-drop on his session with the Menendez boys so she could call the police in case they grew violent. Oziel did what any celebrity would do: he called a press conference.

Now, the story was getting interesting—murder, sex, children killing parents. And so the media played into the sordid twists and turns of a crime story that had endless possibilities.

In March, police arrested Lyle. Erik, who was in Israel, flew back to Miami and was also arrested.

The story changed from a local double homicide to two boys killing their parents, elevating it from local status to the national head-lines. Children turning against their parents, motivated by greed. Those stories do not come along often! In Gibbs's summary, she wrote, "The only relief in sight is that this sideshow will soon be over-shadowed by the main event. . . . At the last hearing the visitors' gallery was packed. Soon it will be the hottest ticket in town, and half the town should be speculating about who should play the various characters when the movie is made. Sean Penn as Lyle? Rob Lowe as Erik? But who should play Judalon Smyth and Oziel?"

On March 26, 1990, in a courtroom packed with reporters, the brothers were arraigned. As if playing to the media, the boys appeared to be smug and arrogant, waving and smiling at their friends and relatives. The media took it all in, later giving it back as sensational headlines for their readers.

The Menendez brothers spent the next three years waiting for their trial. They were housed in the Los Angeles County men's jail in separate cells. This was the same place where O.J. Simpson waited for his trial.

On December 8, 1992, they were indicted on charges that they murdered their parents. Both were eligible for the death penalty.

On May 14, 1993, Judge Stanley Weissberg ruled that both brothers would be tried together, with different juries.

Their defense would be that they were victims of child abuse. The media went crazy. The story was back in the headlines. And once again, the media was used to shape public opinion.

On July 17, 1993, three days before the start of the trial, Leslie Abramson, part of the defense team, gave an interview to the *Los Angles Times* in which she said that a series of increasingly intense confrontations between the brothers and their parents had led to the murders.

According to the Court TV Web site,

> Abramson and Lansing had consulted with Paul Mones, a lawyer and children's rights advocate. Mones had written *When a Child Kills: Abused Children Who Kill Their Parents*, a book that outlines how attorneys can successfully defend children accused of killing their parents. . . . Mones believes that when a parent is murdered, it is their fault.
>
> Abramson and Jill Lansing followed Mones' advice and dressed their clients in boyish sweaters, sport shirts and khaki pants all in an effort to show that Lyle and Erik were not men of 22 and 25, but boys of twelve and fifteen. Abramson wanted to show that Lyle was a boy and that she was his indulgent aunt. Throughout the trial she picked lint off his sweater and she made sure to keep her arm on his shoulder whenever she whispered into his ear. By behaving in this way, Abramson implied that she was not defending a monster, just a misunderstood boy who needed good parenting. (Pergament, 2003)

The arrogant, cocky boys that showed up at the arraignment three years prior were gone.

In this case, Judge Weissberg acknowledged the overwhelming media interest in the case and limited the number of seats in the courtroom. He decided to allow a single television camera in the court-room. It would broadcast the entire trial. What better way to keep the public interest? The print media could not allow competition over the airwaves, so they, too, took to daily coverage.

Playing to the jury and to public opinion, the boys were por-trayed as victims by their attorneys, who did not deny they killed their parents, but said it was their fear of them that caused them to do what they did.

They portrayed Jose as having sexually molested both his boys, an allegation that was never brought up until seven months after the murder.

The defense case lasted three months, with the judge ruling that thirty of their ninety witnesses were not valid. Lyle testified for nine days, saying that at age thirteen he believed his father was molesting his brother. He accused his mother of also sexually abusing him when he was eleven and twelve.

In September, Erik began his testimony. In October, the defense began its attempt to show the jury why the boys believed that they were in danger. At that point, their mother's family had enough, and they turned to a willing media that was covering all the sordid details in order to relate their side of the story.

According to Court TV,

> During this time, Kitty's family began to speak to the news media about the defense and how she was being portrayed. Kitty's brother, Milton Anderson, told his hometown paper, *The Daily SouthTown*, that the brothers' defense was "bull." He believed that Lyle and Erik killed because of greed. He said that the defense visited him and tried to convince him that his sister and brother-in-law were bad people. Anderson told the paper, "My sister didn't abuse her children." Anderson felt that Jose and Kitty had not disciplined their sons enough. (Pergament, 2003)

Judge Weissberg advised the jury that they had four choices: The boys could be found guilty of first-degree murder with special circum-stances; they could be found guilty of second-degree murder; they could be found guilty of voluntary manslaughter; or they could be found guilty of involuntary manslaughter.

After sixteen days of deliberations, on January 13, 1994, Erik's jury said they were deadlocked. On January 25, after twenty-four days of deliberation, Lyle's jury announced it was also deadlocked. Judge Weissberg declared mistrials in both cases.

On February 28, 1995, a new trial date was set for June. That was postponed, and in August 1995, a new trial began, this time with only one jury. There was another major difference in this trial. On October 11, 1995, Judge Weissberg ruled that the trial could not be televised because it would "increase the risk that jurors would be exposed to information and commentary about the case from outside the courtroom."

This was an interesting ruling in that the court acknowledged the potential influence of media coverage in high-profile crimes.

> In a *Simpson* ripple effect, Judge Stanley Weissberg has banned cameras from his Van Nuys courtroom. He has also ruled that the brothers be tried together, as the separate juries last time created too much confusion. Abramson—surprisingly, given her penchant for publicity last time around and her telegenic presence for ABC as an expert commentator on the Simpson case—requested and was denied a gag order to prevent the prosecution or anyone else from talking to TV reporters about the case. The State's new team, headed by deputy district attorney David Conn, insists that this time the prosecution will focus on the murders themselves, rather than get derailed by the defense's claim that Lyle and Erik were sexually and emotionally abused by their parents. (Bleick, 1995)

Bleick went on to state, "No one knows how long this trial will take. Even without a television audience to play to, the lawyers ran into overtime in their opening arguments."

In November, the prosecution rested its case after calling thirty witnesses.

On December 6, Erik began the first of fifteen days of testimony. On January 12, Lyle's attorney changed his defense strategy and told the court he planned to argue that Lyle killed his parents in the heat of passion and that fear and anger overwhelmed him. He did not want Lyle to testify because of damaging impeachment evidence the prosecution had obtained since the first trial that included a letter in which he described how he "snowed" the jury at his first trial and a letter telling his former girlfriend how to testify. On January 30, after twenty-five witnessed testified, the defense rested.

Rebuttal began in February. February 20 was the start of four days of closing arguments for the prosecution. February 26 was the first of three days of closing arguments for the defense. The defense played to the jury by stating that the prosecution presented fraudulent witnesses for political reasons, trying to point out the Los Angeles district attorney's office was under pressure to win a high-profile case after losing the first Menendez trial and the O.J. Simpson murder trial.

Deliberations began on March 1. On March 20, after four days of deliberation, the brothers were convicted of two counts of first-degree murder each, as well as conspiracy to commit murder. Two special circumstances were attached to the murders, lying in wait and multiple murders, which meant only two sentencing options: life in prison without possibility of parole, or death by execution.

On March 22, the penalty phase began and was completed in three weeks. "In his closing argument, Barry Levine accused the Los Angeles County district attorney's office of arbitrarily deciding who was eligible for the death penalty. He reminded the jury of the O.J. Simpson case and said, 'He's not even eligible for the death penalty.' Levine told the jury that the prosecution had not presented evidence of aggravating circumstances other than the crime itself" (Pergament, 2003).

The jury voted for life imprisonment, and the men were sentenced on July 2, 1996.

On January 27, 1997, David Conn was notified he would be transferred to the Norwalk district attorney's office. Following the Menendez verdicts, Conn gave an interview to the *Los Angeles Times*, saying he 'wouldn't mind one day being the Los Angeles district attorney' (Pergament, 2003)

After numerous appeals, the brothers remained in jail. They are each serving two consecutive life prison terms without the possibility of parole. Lyle is being held at the California Correctional Institution at Tehachapi. Erik is at the California State Prison in Sacramento County.

David Conn left the D.A.'s office for private practice.

A three-year investigation by the State Bar of California into Leslie Abramson's behavior during the retrial ended with a ruling of insufficient evidence. And there were, of course, the books.

Don Davis wrote *Bad Blood: The Shocking True Story Behind the Menendez Killings*; Ronald Soble and John Johnson wrote *Blood Brothers: The Inside Story of the Menendez Murders*; Hazel Thornton wrote *Hung Jury: The Diary of a Menendez Juror* (Hazel was a juror—she discusses the gender division that she says happened in the jury that resulted in the hung jury); Paul Mones, a consultant on the trials, wrote *When a Child Kills: Abused Children Who Kill Their Parents*; Alan Dershowitz devoted a chapter to it in his book, *The Abuse Excuse and Other Cop-Outs, Sob Stories and Evasions of Responsibility*; and finally Lyle even got into the act with *In the Private Diary of Lyle Menendez: In His Own Words*, featuring transcripts of conversations between Lyle and Norma Novelli, a friend of his, while he was in the Los Angeles County Men's Jail. Famous crime writer Dominick Dunne also wrote a series of articles about the crimes and trials for *Vanity Fair* magazine.

And lest we forget the TV movies . . . CBS ran *The Beverly Hills Murders*, a movie about the Menendez murders.

Why was the media so fascinated with the story? One explanation:

A disturbing subtext runs through our recent media fixations. Parents abuse sons—allegedly at least, in the Menendez case—who, in turn, rise up and kill them. A husband torments a wife who retaliates with a kitchen knife. Love turns into obsession, between the Simpsons anyway, and then perhaps into a murderous rage: the family, in other words, becomes a personal hell. This accounts for at least part of our fascination with the Bobbitts and the Simpsons and the rest of them. We live in a culture that "fetishizes" the family as the ideal unit of human community, the perfect container for our lusts and loves. (Ehrenreich, 1994)

The first trial also brought a wave of watchers who, instead of being hooked on soap operas, became hooked on live TV. But, according to some experts, that might not always be a bad thing. While docudramas had been the hit of the past, with reality shows now part of everyday coverage, these shows will have to include more of the facts.

The Menendez brothers are now in prison, and the story, like so many others, is no longer being covered in the media. But, like many others, it shows the effects of intense media coverage—the books, the TV docudramas, and the resulting questions—what made this story different from the hundreds, perhaps thousands, of similar cases that happen in this country, but never reach the level of national headlines? Would things have been different for the Menendez brothers if they had not received national attention? Would Erik's confession ever have been made public? Would the second trial have ended differently? There is no way to know what effect being in the national spotlight had on this double homicide case.

## DISCUSSION QUESTIONS

1. Do you think the judge was right in ruling cameras were to be banned in the second trial?
2. What influence do you think the cameras had in the first trial?
3. Does having daily coverage of a trial potentially influence the participants?
4. Why was the public fascinated by this trial?
5. Discuss the pros and cons of having daily televised coverage of trials.

# Colin Ferguson, 1993

Whereas other trials in this book have been noted for their media *over*exposure, the Colin Ferguson trial must be noted for its *under*exposure. It is a clear example of how the media chooses what it will cover, how and when it will cover it, and the amount of space or air time it will allot for coverage. There are no standardized rules, no guidelines, no oversight in what we see in our daily media coverage, and the Colin Ferguson case is just one example of it. The outcome of the trial might not have been different, but theoretically, extended media coverage might have had other effects, including better security on public transportation. Practically, there was no way to tell what would have happened if the Ferguson trial had had extensive publicity. Most people never heard of Colin Ferguson, unlike O.J. Simpson. Yet, while O.J. Simpson went on trial for the murder of his wife and her friend, Colin Ferguson was accused and eventually convicted of a much more horrendous crime, the murder of strangers on a public railroad. His crime affected hundreds of people, but his notoriety was limited to the local area where the crime occurred.

It was a horrific crime—people following a daily routine suddenly faced with a mindless killer. But, unlike similar stories, this incident is a study in why, when seemingly it *should have had* national coverage, it only made local headlines.

December 7, 1993. It was a normal rush hour in New York City as tired commuters jammed the 5:33 P.M. eastbound train on the Long Island Railroad to head home after their busy workday. None of the commuters took any special notice as Colin Ferguson, a

**45**

thirty-seven-year-old Jamaican native, entered the train and took the window seat in the southwestern part of the third car. As the commuters settled in, many began to close their eyes for a quick nap, while others began to read to pass the time. There was no hint that this commute would be different from the hundreds they took every year. Approximately thirty minutes after the train left Penn Station, just after 6:00 P.M., it arrived in New Hyde Park, halfway into its commute into the heart of Nassau County, an eastern suburban region of New York City.

It was at this point that Ferguson had carefully planned to commit his crime. As the train pulled away from the New Hyde Park Station, Ferguson calmly got up from his seat and aimed a 9-mm semiautomatic Ruger pistol, loaded with black Talon bullets that were designed to expand on impact. He fired his first shot into the chest of a female passenger seated across the aisle from him. He then walked in an easterly direction, emptying his first clip of fifteen rounds before he approached the first vestibule. His bullets had already wounded seven passengers and killed three others. The quiet commute had become a nightmarish scene, filled with horrified screams and gunsmoke. Panicked passengers tried desperately to escape the death car, while others stayed in their seats pretending to be dead. Passengers acted on instinct, fed by sheer panic.

Ferguson then took a few steps back to his seat, where he had left his bag. He dropped the empty clip on the floor and reloaded his gun. He turned, the gun clasped in both hands, and deliberately moved his straightened arms to the left and right, shooting passengers as he headed again in an easterly direction.

A river of blood began to flow down the floor of the railroad car. As the random carnage continued, more innocent passengers were killed or seriously wounded. His second clip of ammunition was now empty. He tried again to reload, but this time it would be more difficult.

A group of passengers took quick advantage of the pause in his shooting spree and grabbed him, stopping the deadly rampage. What makes some people victims, some immobilized by fear, and others heroes may never be explained. But, when it was all over, six passengers were dead, nineteen others seriously injured. If the passengers hadn't stopped Ferguson, there is no doubt the death toll would have been much higher. In his bag were two more fully loaded clips plus eighty additional rounds of ammunition. A normal commute, which millions of people across the county take daily, randomly turned deadly. It is a nightmare that could happen anywhere, at any time. But it did not occur until that day on Long Island. And then it became real and it changed lives forever.

It is a story that, under normal circumstances, would attract national attention from its outset. Even the bizarre trial would have attracted national media attention. But not in this case. The trial was left virtually uncovered by the national media. In this case, the national media was busy elsewhere.

The story was left for the local media to cover, and they did. They spent their time dissecting the crime, looking for new angles and new ways to cover it, while the national media continued to ignore the story.

Locally, the politicians took advantage. In a spontaneous re-action to the horrific crime, then County Executive Thomas Gulotta said, "The person who committed this crime is an animal who turned that Long Island Railroad car into a death chamber." While this is an apparently normal reaction to an unthinkable act, calling Ferguson an animal did not sit well with some black activists.

Soon after, Jesse Jackson shot back, saying it was a racial remark. In *Newsday* he was quoted as saying, "This is no time to pour salt on the wounds of the grieving and to expand the fear. His comments were immature and inappropriate. We should not resort to name calling and stereotyping" (Young & Mintz, 2003).

In that same story, Gulotta shot back, defending his comments as nonracist: "It's time that we stopped mincing words about criminals. My heart went out to the victims and the families. . . . My response to that was a purely emotional and human response and I would have expressed that feeling with regard to anyone of any race who had massacred innocent victims and brought so much pain and suffering on the victims and families." He added, "Actually I have greater respect for animals than I do for that killer. Animals only kill for a reason. He very clearly indiscriminately killed innocent human beings for no reason."

For days, the local newspapers played up the controversy. Jackson went to Garden City where the shootings occurred and held a prayer session. Gulotta refused to go. Once again, the focus was shifting away from the victims, as the media, always looking for new angles, focused on a new controversy.

Even Al Sharpton got into the fray. Sharpton accused the media of portraying blacks as inciting Ferguson. "For people in the media to attempt to demonize black dissatisfaction and black rage by say-ing that this man is in some way inspired or condoned by us when he did a very sick and perverted act is really unfair," Sharpton told reporters. He then attacked the media for featuring interviews with residents who accused him of aggravating racial tensions and went on to be quoted as saying, "The press jumped to make it a racial incident and to blame people like us who ourselves have been the victims of violence rather than to deal with the fact that [Ferguson] is a sick man" (Koch, 1993).

The conflict continued as Gulotta spoke with talk show host Howard Stern, defending his remarks. Jackson said he compared Gulotta with Alabama's former segregationist governor, George Wallace, and Arkansas' former segregationist governor, Orval Faubus: "We are urging the county executive to stop referring to people as animals. Its connotation is racial and demeaning" (Young, 2003, p. 21).

Gulotta also appeared on the *Donahue* television show and gave numerous media interviews to the national press. As a result, the press then focused on his political future and began to speculate on a run for governor of New York.

The local media train continued to roll in all directions. Mitchel Moss, director of the Urban Research Center at New York University, wrote,

> The massacre on the Long Island Railroad last week kicked off New York's 1994 gubernatorial campaign. Crime and punishment will be to New York's electorate what taxes were to New Jersey voters in 1993. Since the tragedy in Garden City, politicians have flooded the public with proposals for gun licensing, taxes on ammunition, police on commuter trains, and that old favorite, the death penalty. (Moss, 1993)

While the local press played out the public controversy, the victims' families privately grieved. Fear continued to affect millions of people in the New York area, who no longer felt safe performing their daily routines. While the media focused on political stories, the average person was more concerned about safety.

The real local circus began when Ferguson was brought to trial.

In January 1995, most television sets across the country were tuned into the O.J. Simpson trial in Los Angeles. While the headlines were filled with the trial's events of the day, another trial in New York took backstage, and aside from mostly local coverage, did not evoke massive media attention.

O.J. Simpson, because he was a celebrity, took center stage.

Although one crime was allegedly committed against a spouse and her friend, the other was much more brutal, more horrifying, and left twenty-five innocent victims dead or seriously injured. It was the trial of Colin Ferguson.

Two defendants—two types of coverage. One defendant was famous, the other wanted to be. To a logical mind, it seems unthinkable that one trial could receive all the attention, simply because the defendant was famous, when the second trial affected so many more people. Even the implication that it could have happened anywhere, to anyone, at any time, would normally take center stage. But not this time. Adding to this, Ferguson defended himself, making the trial even more newsworthy.

William M. Kunstler and Ronald L. Kuby initially took on Ferguson's case. They first attempted to use a "black rage" defense, arguing that years of living in an oppressive, race-biased society had affected his mind in such a way that he was not acting willfully when he opened fire. Ferguson disagreed with what they planned and dismissed them. He planned to argue that he had been framed, and someone else had committed the shootings. He would take on his own defense. There would be days of arguments over his ability to handle his own defense, and if he was sane or not.

Nationally, the story continued to be ignored in favor of the O.J. trial, but the local media could not get enough of the daily events where an accused killer was defending himself. It was difficult even for the detectives on the case.

"As homicide detectives, we are accustomed to being questioned by defense attorneys," said Brian Parpan, the lead detective on the case. "I found it demeaning to be at the other end of a mass murderer. There was no question of his guilt and no question of his competency, but still I had to remain professional and still portray to a jury that professionalism. It was difficult."

His colleague, Detective Gary Abbondandelo, agreed. "What made this one really different is that you spend five or six hours with this guy questioning him, and then he is questioning us in the third person, referring to himself as 'the suspect' or 'Mr. Ferguson,' and removing himself from the whole thing and entering now as a lawyer who wasn't there and knows nothing about what we are talking about."

He added, "Another difficult part was that the judge gave him a lot more latitude than a professional attorney would get, as far as his questioning. You would look at the prosecution and wait for an objection that never came. They weren't as picky as with an attorney. I kept waiting for objections that never came and then had to answer the question."

The local press, fascinated by this trial, kept daily updates as well as cameras in the courtroom. This was indeed a unique trial, a mass murderer defending himself—questioning the people he shot. And while it does not take away from a double homicide, can there really be a comparison when not only the number of people murdered and injured is greater, not only does the crime itself affect millions more, but the trial is so bizarre in and of itself? What would make the media ignore this trial in favor of O.J.? Do First Amendment rights guarantee the right of the media to pick and choose what people should know about?

One of the rare national articles written appeared in *Time* magazine, which acknowledged the uniqueness of the trial: "The man who argues his own case, goes the lawyer's bromide, has a fool for a client. But if a client is truly a fool—or worse than that, is insane—then no folksy admonition will stop him, and neither, at least in the Ferguson trial's first week, would his presiding judge" (Van Biema, 1995).

The article goes on to show how truly bizarre the trial was.

> That set the stage for last week's production of Jekyll and Hyde Visit Bleak House. Ferguson's courtly legalisms—*"Did there come a time . . . "* and *"Is it your testimony that . . . "*—and his formal complaints of *"Hearsay!"* or *"Leading the witness!"* chimed very oddly with the preposterousness of his core thesis, expressed in an eerie third person: "The evidence will show that Colin Ferguson was, in fact, a well-meaning passenger on the train . . . Like any other passenger, he dozed off—having the weapon in a bag. At that point someone . . . took the weapon out of the bag and proceeded to shoot."

Ferguson would continually question the credibility of the detectives, accusing them of everything from lying to threatening him with a gun. His demeanor would change from hesitant to superior, from arrogant to accusatory, and from aggressor to victim. He tried to prove that he was a victim of an FBI conspiracy, and in a final plea for sympathy told the jury, "Vindicate Mr. Ferguson. Do not destroy his life more than it has already been destroyed. He has suffered."

His suffering would continue, because the jury convicted him. After he was convicted, many of the victims who were forced to be questioned by him took the stand during the sentencing hearing. They all asked the judge for the maximum sentence. The emotional devastation that surrounded the victims spread quickly. All the months of suppressed rage and anger, of sadness and grief, were over, and as the survivors spoke, others, including the prosecutors and the detectives, cried.

Colin Ferguson was sentenced to consecutive terms of twenty-five years to life for six murders. Ferguson left Long Island the day after his sentencing. It has been estimated that the cost of his trial, the police investigation, and his jail stay for the fifteen months was approximately $1 million. And still the national media did not seem to care.

The death penalty for New York became another issue the local media focused on, and the local politicians as well as the governor's office got on board.

Under any other circumstances, this bizarre trial would have made daily national headlines. Once again, celebrity status appears to drive the force of the media coverage. What local coverage there was did have an unusual secondary effect. Carolyn McCarthy, a nurse from Mineola, whose husband was killed and whose son was seriously injured, became an advocate for gun control. The local publicity from the case was her stepping-stone into a career as a congresswoman.

Was she elected on her merits, or did the local media help change her status as a victim into that of a heroine? Certainly she would never have considered a role as congresswoman. She ran on one major issue—gun control. Does repeated exposure combined with the sympathy angle project an image that propels an ordinary citizen into the political arena?

After the massacre, the death penalty was established in New York State.[1] A TV movie was made about the massacre and aired in 1998.

Colin Ferguson's crime and his trial has left an important legacy for media analysts. The most important question, perhaps, is: How can the coverage of O.J. Simpson be justified against the almost non-existent coverage of Colin Ferguson? The question, as always, is: What price for being a celebrity?

## DISCUSSION QUESTIONS

1. Should the trial of Colin Ferguson have gotten more coverage, and if so, why?

2. Why do you think the national media chose to virtually ignore this case?

3. Compare this case to others in this book and decide why the media covers some cases so completely and ignores others.

4. Would there have been a different outcome if the case had received more coverage?

5. Why do you think no books were written on this case?

---

[1]It has since been declared unconstitutional in New York and there is no death penalty.

# The O.J. Simpson Case, 1994

It was known as the trial of the century, but it was the status of the alleged killer that turned the trial into a frenzy of media coverage. Unknown people involved in the trial became stars overnight, and the daily news reports took precedence over most other news. The coverage even spread overseas, where it seemed no one could get enough information.

It was the media that pushed this trial into the spotlight, and in the end, it was the media that appeared to influence its outcome. In a sense, the American public became part of the jury as both the prosecutor and the defense played not only to the jury, but to the media as well. The daily coverage drew millions of viewers, and few were without an opinion even before the trial began.

It's an easy case to recognize. The defendant became so famous he was known throughout the country by his initials. His name is Orenthal James Simpson, O.J. was always known as O.J. from his time playing pro football.

Although the murder of an ex–football star's wife brought its own publicity, it was when O.J. became a suspect that the media went wild. And what more could add to the hype than a slow chase covered live in which O.J. appeared to be fleeing police.

On June 17, O.J.'s lawyers were notified that an arrest warrant was being issued. What followed would have made a perfect movie script.

At 6:45 P.M., an Orange County sheriff spotted O.J.'s Bronco on Interstate 5 in California. He ordered it to pull over, but the driver, Al Cowling, a longtime friend of O.J.'s, refused. He put on his hazard lights and slowed to 40 miles per hour. He then dialed 911 on his cell phone and told police that they should back off and that O.J. was suicidal and had a gun to his head.

Of course, the media had been alerted, and helicopters filled the skies above the car. This slow-speed chase became the most widely watched impromptu "TV show" in the history of American television. Spectators, alerted by the media, gathered along the freeway, shouting and cheering. A circus atmosphere ensued. Cowling asked to go to O.J.'s house, and the cavalcade passed into the jurisdiction of Los Angeles police.

At 8:45 P.M., O.J. emerged from the car at his home. Above him, like moths drawn to a flame, were dozens of helicopters. Across the nation, millions of viewers were watching the bizarre scene, a sign of things to come.

O.J. was arrested. Even though he spent the 15 months after his arrest in a small jail cell, the publicity surrounding his trial quickly spread across the nation and the world, reaching millions of people. The trial began on January 23, 1995, with the People of the State of California, Plaintiff, versus Orenthal James Simpson, Defendant, in Los Angeles County Superior Court.

The trial was the longest in the history of the state of California, and cost more than $20 million. More than 2,000 reporters covered the story for twenty-three newspapers and magazines. There were daily video feeds from 121 locations for nineteen television stations and eight radio stations. At any time of the day or night, a television or radio station would be covering the story. Almost every major newspaper did daily updates. The participants in the trial became instant celebrities, and research indicated that although 74 percent of Americans were able to identify Kato Kaelin, only 25 percent knew who Vice President Al Gore was.

Referred to as "The Trial of the Century," the case received more coverage and hype than any other criminal trial since the Lindbergh kidnapping and murder case in the 1930s. The results of this constant coverage soon became obvious. The lawyers began to play not only to the jury, but to the public as well. The prosecutor, Marcia Clark, changed her hairstyle continually throughout the trial, seemingly as concerned about her appearance as her prosecution.

O.J.'s defense team became known as the "dream team," basking in the daily media attention. Unattainable by the average person, the group was costing O.J. thousands of dollars every week. The lawyers were known for their ability to attract media attention, but had little experience defending clients against murder charges. With all this media attention, it seemed few people were asking a basic question: What happened to Nicole Brown Simpson and Ronald Goldman? Who had killed them?

It was clear the two victims were taking a back seat to the man who was becoming bigger than life, a man who began his trial by responding, after being asked what he pled, "Absolutely, one hundred percent, not guilty!" No one questioned how much time the media spent on the victims; instead it seemed as if no one could get enough of O.J.

What made this trial so important? It was even reported that one study estimated U.S. industry lost more than $25 billion as workers left their jobs to concentrate on the trial. It is estimated that 91 percent of the viewing audience watched parts of the trial, and 142 million listened on the radio and watched television when the verdict was read.

Who was this man who fascinated the American public? He had once been a famous football player, winning the Heisman Trophy as the top college football player in 1968. He played for the Buffalo Bills and won sports records, including most rushing yards gained in one season, most rushing gained in a single game, and most touchdowns scored in a season. In 1979, he had retired, and the public then knew him for his commercials for a rental car company. But after the murders, the subsequent media attention, and the public's apparent fascination with the trial, he became more than just a famous football player. He was the center of everyday media stories, the person who made the daily headlines, and the man whom everyone was talking about.

As a result, there were serious repercussions from this continuous media hype. Perhaps the most serious was the effect in minority communities, where the trial was seen by many as not about guilt or innocence, but more about whether a black man could find justice in a mostly white-dominated legal system. This was an obvious ploy based on the actions of the defense "dream team."

In his opening statement, the late Johnnie Cochran, a member of the team, quoted from Martin Luther King, Jr., saying "injustice anywhere is a threat to justice everywhere." He then told the mostly black jury that they would act as the conscience of the community and when the trial was over, they would have to return there.

On the other side, there were whites who would question whether a mostly minority jury could come back with a guilty conviction against a black celebrity. It became clear early on in the trial that the group of highly paid, high-powered defense attorneys were going to continue to use the race card in their attempt to prove their client's innocence.

Throughout the trial, the media attention never faulted. It was as if the country had nothing else that was newsworthy, as every major newspaper kept the trial as one of its lead headlines. "The court of public opinion may be one of America's most maligned institutions. But in every high-profile case, it's still the place where everybody goes to plead. So with the nation largely—and, for the most part, miserably—poised between affection for O.J. Simpson and the revulsion at the bloody slicing of Nicole Simpson and Ron Goldman, a public game is in play between O.J.'s accusers and his defenders" (Lacayo, 1994). The daily television coverage fueled the media hype. On January 24, Judge Lance Ito apparently had enough. "A furious Judge Lance Ito abruptly recessed the O.J. Simpson trial at the end of the afternoon to consider whether to pull the plug on live TV coverage of the trial, after the faces of two jurors were glimpsed during a portion of today's coverage" (*Time*, 1995). But, through all this, nothing compared to the days spent waiting for the jury's verdict.

The police presence, already evident throughout the trial, was multiplied and news helicopters flew over the area. Hundreds more police were on call, the justice department had a plan to coordinate federal assistance if needed, and even the president had been briefed. The power of the media was never more evident as it was the day the country seemed to hold its breath waiting for the final verdict.

On Friday, September 29, Judge Ito issued his final instructions to the jury, telling them not to begin their actual deliberations until the following Monday. That Monday the jury started at a little past nine in the morning. Five hours later they notified Judge Ito that they had reached a verdict. Judge Ito made it known that he would not disclose that verdict until the following morning.

On Tuesday morning, O.J. was declared not guilty and became a free man. Reactions from the black communities were relief and joy, from the white communities, frustration. Networks overseas showed the verdicts, and many believed racism was on trial in America. In the end, the effect of the news media became even more apparent, because the trial had many legacies. While some questioned the role of the media in court cases, there were also questions about the role of money and celebrity status in the legal system. There were also questions about race relations and domestic violence. There were also questions about the effect of cameras in the courtroom.

## WHAT MADE THIS CASE DRAW DAILY COVERAGE?

It is not just Simpson's fame that made his one of the most relentlessly reported cases ever. Hoping to overcome O.J.'s advantage in public sympathy—unusual for an accused killer—city officials and police played to the media every step of the way. "The flood of sometimes inaccurate leaks from police about bloody gloves and a ski mask was followed by a heavy round of appearances on public affairs shows by Garcetti. . . . 'The prosecution is in the unusual position of having to try to shape public opinion its way,' says Charles Weisselberg, a criminal law expert at the University of Southern California" (Lacayo, 1994).

And then there were the legacies of the key players in the trial, most of whom no one knew before the trial. With their continuous presence throughout the trial in newspapers and on television, many made the conscious effort to cash in on their fame by writing books and staying in the public eye as long as the public would have them.

Marcia Clark, the chief prosecutor who kept changing her hairstyle, also changed her career. She wrote a book, *Without a Doubt*, and reportedly received $4 million for it, although sales reportedly did not meet expectations. The book also was said to upset Nicole's sister, Denise Brown, who felt the contents were not accurate. Clark no longer practices law; her plans for her own television show apparently did not materialize; but she does appear regularly as a guest host on *Rivera Live*, a show on CNBC.

Christopher Darden, who was Marcia Clark's co-counsel, beat her to the bookstores and co-authored a book, titled *In Contempt*, for a reported $1.3 million. He also beat her in sales, making it to the best-seller list. Later, Darden also co-wrote a series of thrillers. He is now a defense attorney, teaches law, and appears on television as a commentator.

Johnnie Cochran Jr., O.J.'s lawyer (recently deceased), might always be known for his quote about the bloody glove found at the scene: "If it doesn't fit, you must acquit," which he later said was suggested by another member of the legal team, Gerald Uelmen (Liptak, 2005). Cochran took advantage of the fame he achieved during the trial and opened a national law firm that was devoted mainly to personal injury cases. He wrote two books, *A Lawyer's Life* and *Journey to Justice*, hosted a cable television show, did legal commentaries on

NBC, and played himself on a soap opera. He died of a brain tumor in March 2005.

Robert Shapiro, the lawyer who put together the "dream team," wrote a book about the case, *Search for Justice*. He later defended music producer Phil Spector and Darryl Strawberry. He also co-founded a company that sells legal forms.

Kato Kaelin played himself on a reality show and did radio spots. He also worked in comedy development for National Lampoon.

Mark Fuhrman, the detective who was accused of racial bias and who found the bloody glove, became a broadcast analyst and wrote *Murder in Brentwood*, followed by *Murder in Greenwich* about a decade-old unsolved murder. He also hosted a radio talk show.

Judge Lance Ito tried many cases after O.J.'s, but did not allow TV cameras in the courtroom.

Faye Resnick, Nicole Simpson's close friend, wrote two books about the case and posed for *Playboy*.

Two of the Los Angeles police detectives, Tom Lange and Philip Vannatter, retired after the trial and wrote the best-selling book, *Evidence Dismissed*.

Fred Goldman, father of murdered Ron Goldman, worked as a special assistant on victim's rights and then pursed a career in broadcasting. The Goldmans and their daughter Kim wrote a book, *His Name Is Ron*.

Nicole's sister, Denise, heads the Nicole Brown Charitable Foundation, which helps battered women.

In a civil suit that received much less publicity, the victims' families sued O.J. Requiring a lesser standard of proof, the jury found him liable for the murders and ordered him to pay $33.5 million. The family also sued for custody of the Simpson children.

But problems came with that as well: "The Browns, however, had their own behavior to defend in the custody case. It was revealed that Louis Brown had earned $262,000 since his daughter's death by selling her diary to the *National Enquirer* and the home video of her wedding to a television tabloid show. In addition, sister Dominique confessed that she had sold topless photos of Nicole to the *National Enquirer*" (Lafferty, 1997).

The media continued its coverage of the civil trial, exploiting every detail: "But it has not been without its moments, including Mr. Simpson's taking the stand for the first time, the judge's ruling that race could not be made a major issue in the case and the plaintiffs' suddenly producing 30 photographs that raised fresh doubts about Mr. Simpson's contention that he did not kill his former wife" (Ayres, 1997).

On the Web site Famous American Trials, O.J.'s is well described:

> Although the 1995 criminal trial of O.J. Simpson for the murders of
> Nicole Brown Simpson and Ronald Goldman has been called "a great
> trash novel come to life," no one can deny the pull it had on the Amer-
> ican public. If the early reports of the murder of the wife of the ex-NFL
> football star (turned NBC sports announcer) hadn't caught people's full
> attention, Simpson's surreal Bronco ride on the day of his arrest cer-
> tainly did—ninety-five million television viewers witnessed the slow
> police chase live. The 133 days of televised courtroom testimony turned
> countless viewers into Simpson trial junkies. Even foreign leaders such
> as Margaret Thatcher and Boris Yeltsin eagerly gossiped about the trial.
> When Yeltsin stepped off his plane to meet President Clinton, the first
> question he asked was, "Do you think O.J. did it?" (Linder, 2000)

The civil trial did not bring as much publicity, party because it
was not televised, and the participants were under a court order not
to discuss the proceedings with the media. The settlement remains
unpaid. Because he now lives in Florida, O.J.'s pension goes un-
touched, and he has been quoted as saying he feels no obligation to
pay because he did not commit the murders.

But for some, there were lessons to be learned from the trial:

> If O.J. Simpson is a free man today, he leaves behind a machinery of law
> that looks as twisted as any Los Angeles freeway after an earthquake.
> Critics of his acquittal point to issues that took the trial where it had no
> business going, from the defense plea for racial reparations to breath-
> less news bulletins on Marcia Clark's hairdo. Yet even within the strict
> letter of the law, the case unfolded with such grotesque distortions of
> what most Americans think of as normal justice that the system itself
> ended up in the dock. Verdicts are now coming down, and they are not
> pretty. From police irregularities to the issue of trial by jury itself, what
> the British writer G. K. Chesterton called "the awful court of judgment"
> has acquired a modern spin on the adjective. (Walsh, 1995)

In the end, Thomas L. Jones, a writer for the Web site Court TV's
crime library, summed up the trial: "By the time it was all over, it had
long ceased to be about law and order and justice served, and instead
had become about voyeurs feasting on and being titillated by the
complex lifestyles and tragedies of people whose lives, loves and,
ultimately, deaths simply served up a special brand of entertainment
to help a bored audience get through the day."

Jones also wrote that O.J. still insists on his innocence: "He also
complained that the media was responsible for making the public
believe that he murdered his wife. He hopes that the real killer is
found some day so he can prove people wrong."

The media also began to analyze the role of television in the courtroom. Citing Gerald Uelmen, a Santa Clara University law dean who served on the Simpson team, *Time* magazine looked at the impact. "Uelmen agrees that the 'entertainment medium' took command: 'We had witnesses who treated their testimony like a gig. We had witnesses who were afraid to testify, who were afraid of what it would do to their reputations.' But, adds Uelmen, 'evidence was uncovered because of television coverage. All those photos of O.J. wearing gloves at football games, for example, came from volunteers' " (Walsh, 1995).

And like so many other trials, O.J.'s left an unusual legacy. "What happened to the once seemingly inexorable march of cameras into the courtroom? The answer, most trial watchers agree, boils down to two initials: O.J. His obsessively covered trial in 1995—and the subsequent criticism of Judge Lance Ito's handling of the proceedings— has made nearly every judge presiding over a high-profile case opt for the safer, camera-free route" (Zoglin, 2005).

In the years following the trial, other questions were brought up as well. "The O.J. Simpson trial kicked off this new era . . . and the sensational stories that followed, from JonBenet Ramsey to Monica Lewinsky to Elian Gonzalez (and all his dysfunctional relatives), . . . fit the mold of news-as-argument: Everyone had to take a position on who was right and who was beneath contempt. From the kidnapping of Elizabeth Smart to whether Chandra Levy was having an affair with a congressman to whether Scott Peterson murdered his wife, television has tirelessly flogged tragedies that once would have been purely local crime stories" (Kurtz, 2005, p. BO1).

All of which again brings up the question of why O.J. was so well covered nationally and a case like Colin Ferguson's was not. Is it the media that makes the crime, or the crime that makes the media?

## DISCUSSION QUESTIONS

1. What role did O.J.'s status as a sports hero play in the coverage of the trial?
2. How did O.J.'s status as a sports hero affect public opinion?
3. What were the factors that contributed to this murder trial becoming the "trial of the century"?
4. Why did race become a factor in this trial?
5. Did Marcia Clark's playing to the media affect the outcome of the trial?

# 10

# JonBenet Ramsey, 1996

It has been established that there are no guidelines as to what story the media will choose to highlight. Certainly, a child killer makes headlines. But what made the difference in the case of JonBenet Ramsey? Sadly, it was not just the fact that a child was found murdered. It was the media finding a news story that supplied headlines at a time when there was no other news going on; it was a cute young girl packaged by home videos of her beauty pageants; and it was the holiday time of year.

And so the story leaped into the national headlines and stayed there for years to come. Should it have taken such precedence over other similar cases? If none of these factors were present, the media might have ignored it. It was clearly the media that chose to make it into the story it became, and it was the media that influenced not only the investigation, but possibly the ability of the true killer to escape capture.

JonBenet—there are few people in this country and overseas that do not know that name. It is a heartbreaking story. From the moment it was made public, all the facts became media events, taking on lives of their own; lives based on the tragic death of a six-year-old little girl.

It happened during one of the slowest news times of the year. Many people were on vacation, celebrating the holidays.

A small child, murdered in her own home on Christmas Day, was news. And the footage of JonBenet, dancing, in a pink sequined dress, singing, "I wanna be a cowboy's sweetheart" began to hit the news and was picked up by the tabloids. The media sources, such as the AP, *The Globe, The National Enquirer,* and every other piece of journalism picked up the story and attached every ugly headline they could think of to it.

. . . The media basically went mad for JonBenet. A 6-year-old beauty queen is kidnapped, molested, and murdered in her own home. This was the best kind of tabloid journalism and was made for the opportunists' advantage by cashing in on the name of JonBenet. (Griffy, 2002)

The story began in December 1996, when JonBenet's body was found in the basement of her home in Colorado. Her father, John, ran a successful computer company. Her mother, Patsy, was a former beauty queen. They lived in a large home in an elite suburb of Boulder.

The three had been to a Christmas party and had returned home after 9:30 P.M. Patsy told police that JonBenet had fallen asleep in the car, so they carried her to her room and put her to bed. They had planned to get up early to take a trip to their vacation home at Lake Michigan. At 5:00 A.M., according to her mother, she found a ransom note on the stairs. She checked to find JonBenet missing. Police records show a call was made to 911 at 5:25 A.M.

From that point on, mass confusion ensued. The police department was later accused by numerous sources of doing a shoddy investigation. The crime scene was not immediately secured, and later was contaminated by the Ramseys and their friends.

JonBenet's murder—particularly as the days went by and no arrests were forthcoming—quickly became a national obsession, featured day after day on network news, television tabloid programs, talk radio, newspapers and magazines. . . . Her unusual first name became so well known that like Cher and Madonna, she no longer had need of a last name. The public's shock at the murder soon began to share equal time with its growing dismay at the Boulder Police's investigation, a dismay fed by a steady stream of leaks from the Boulder County District Attorney's office about the inept police investigation being conducted. (Maloney & O'Connor, 1999)

The story went on to say that in addition to the crime scene not being sealed off, "it appeared the police were treating the primary suspects—JonBenet's parents—with kid gloves by not only acquiescing to their refusal to be interviewed at police headquarters, but also to being interviewed separately. Fueled with such information, the media, especially the tabloid television and talk radio shows, were showing no such restraint toward the glamorous child's parents" (Maloney & O'Connor).

The day after the body was found, John and Patsy hired separate attorneys. When police questioned his son, daughter, and ex-wife, John then hired attorneys for them as well.

With no immediate arrests, the story continued to grow. The media could not get enough of it. By December 27, reporters, like animals hovering over their prey, became impatient that neither the Ramseys nor their friends would talk to them. They questioned what they were hiding.

Brian Cabell put a perspective on the national coverage in *Perfect Murder, Perfect Town:*

> During the final days of '96, I read about a little girl who had been murdered in Colorado—JonBenet Ramsey. I worked in Atlanta for CNN as the network's Southeast correspondent. In the news business, it was the sort of story you'd quickly dismiss—it didn't have a national feel to it. But when it emerged that the child had been a beauty pageant queen, the story became sexier. That's what we played up. (Schiller, 1999)

Here we have the first glimpse of what makes a news story worthy of national attention: Just make it sexy. That and more were all part of this story as more events unfolded. On December 29, four days after the murder, a memorial service was held. On December 30, the Ramseys returned to Atlanta to bury JonBenet. The funeral was held on New Year's Eve, 1996.

At that time, the Ramseys had agreed to do an interview on CNN. The interview was aired New Year's Day. Steve Thomas, one of the lead investigators on the case, who wrote *JonBenet: Inside the Ramsey Murder Investigation*, said it was the first time the Ramseys broke their silence since the death of their daughter, and that they did it with the media, instead of talking with the police.

> Arranging an interview with a news organization was a tactic they would use repeatedly in coming years, and, in my opinion, it was always sheer propaganda, allowing them to spin a public relations story while avoiding the police. Most of the time the reporters involved agreed in advance not to ask them anything about the murder of their daughter. And the reporters, however well informed, knew only a fraction of the real case. Cops wanted to ask tougher, deeper questions. (Thomas & Davis, 2000)

But Thomas was not the only one who questioned these actions. Reporters felt as if they were being manipulated and asked the logical questions: Why a staged interview? Why didn't the Ramseys answer the questions of the local reporters who were camped out in Boulder? Why would they not talk to the reporters who had been following the case and were more closely aware of the facts?

The media fury increased with the release of an enhanced 911 tape. It contradicted the story that the Ramseys told police, that their son Burke was asleep when Patsy found the note and later made the call. By January 4, the media was running stories that JonBenet had been strangled with a garrote, that she had a fractured skull, that the ransom note was written on paper already in the home, and just how much ransom was demanded. The police accused the district attorney's office of leaking the information, and the district attorney's office accused the police of a sloppy investigation.

On January 4, the Ramseys appeared at their church in a carefully orchestrated media event. Their press representative had the congregation leave by the front door, not the usual side door. The press, eager for any news and tipped off by the Ramseys agent, was waiting outside the door. They got their story. According to Schiller, the photos of the Ramseys appeared on the front page of all the local papers. When Alex Hunter, the district attorney, saw the newspapers and TV coverage, he wondered if the Ramseys were getting good advice. "His common sense told him that people don't behave this way in deep mourning. The scene at the church looked staged and raised questions in his mind about the Ramseys' role in their daughter's death" (Schiller).

The purpose, many felt, was to help create an image of a grieving mother and father. On January 9, a rumor began circulating that John Ramsey had confessed. That night, Police Chief Koby scheduled a press conference. He picked the reporters who were allowed inside the room, ignoring the national press and some local writers. The majority of the press had to wait outside in the lobby.

> Excluding the national media was a huge mistake since the case was the focus of worldwide attention. Anytime you turned on the TV, in Miami or Anchorage, Bangor or San Diego, there was JonBenet parading on stage in provocative clothing and poses. Every newspaper in the land carried stories almost daily and commentators filled the airwaves with opinions. Our chief of police, with his long hair and beard, consistently failed to understand the media. (Thomas & Davis)

Thomas went on to blame Chief Koby for many of the attacks on the police, saying the detectives who were watching the press conference were surprised at his actions:

> Instead of *using* the press, Koby attacked it! "I have never, in the twenty-eight years I have been in this business, seen such media focus on an event. It is intrusive and making it much more difficult to work through this situation. . . . The less you know, the easier it is to give advice." . . . Angry at him, the indignant media came after us harder than ever. (Thomas & Davis)

Chief Koby criticized the media for its obsession with the case and announced he would not allow the case to be tried in the media. Cooperation among the media and the police, the district attorney's office, and residents of Boulder was virtually nonexistent.

The following day, pictures of JonBenet's autopsy began to circulate. On January 13, *The Globe* published photos of what they said was the murder scene. They had also published the autopsy photos. As the tabloids used their money to buy whatever information they could, the mainstream media found themselves without a story. The competition escalated. *Extra* and *Hard Copy* tried to get the Ramseys' housekeeper, Linda Pugh, on their show. She refused. When the *National Enquirer* left a note under her door offering her $20,000 and a trip to Florida, she took it (Schiller).

The press wanted to speak to Pugh, but it appeared that would take money. According to Detective Thomas, "The press was ready to pounce as soon as we walked out of the Pughs' home. When we had entered, only a lone media sentinel was staking out the place, but when we left, there must have been a hundred news people waiting for us" (Thomas & Davis). News stories appeared, reporting that police said JonBenet had been sexually abused.

According to crimelibrary.com, in a story written by Patrick Bellamy, "Mainstream journalists followed the tabloids. Any mention of the Ramseys attracted readers and pushed up ratings."

> When John and Patsy Ramsey appeared on national television New Year's Day, John Ramsey announced he wanted to hire "the best mind this country has to offer" to find his daughter's killers. Since then, the family has fulfilled that promise—assembling a team of lawyers, investigators, a former FBI agent, a media consultant, and even a handwriting expert. . . . The "Ramsey Team" has attracted attention because of the number of high-profile experts on it. (Zaret, 1997)

Pat Corten, a crisis management expert from Washington, D.C., according to the story, was hired to be the family's spokesperson and answered up to 200 media calls daily. They also set up a World Wide Web page. The local papers reported on the so-called secrecy that surrounded the case. "The investigation is also a case study in the interests that collide in any unsolved murder case. The public wants to know everything, while the police don't want to release anything they feel will harm their case" (Brennan, 1997). The story goes on to quote experts who argued both sides of the issue, one stating the public has the right to know all the facts, another that while the public may have that right, they do not have it during the investigative process. In

March, Pat Corten, the Ramseys public relations representative, was fired, and a local person was hired. The district attorney's office and police department tried to keep up with the press.

Both the police and district attorney's office were getting calls from the national media, who made it clear that they would stay in town until the case was solved. ABC reportedly spent $150,000 a month to keep five producers in Boulder. CNN had an entire studio fully equipped with hundreds of videotapes and an editing room located at a local hotel. After a while, both Hunter and his chief assistant, Bill Wise, were spending at least five hours a day just talking to the media, while the chief of police avoided media contact.

The murder of JonBenet was less than two months old, and the investigators were spending their time satisfying the needs of the media. In the beginning of 1997, by putting JonBenet's name into an internet search engine, a person could get between three hundred and a thousand hits. In March, both the local media and the national media began an almost daily criticism of the police investigation.

"The attacks were excruciating. What made them worse was the continued silence of Chief Koby. With no one speaking up for them—and strict instructions that they were not to speak to the media—the officers were frustrated and angry. Officers who wanted the Ramsey case prosecuted without delay and were willing to ignore the presumption of innocence realized that the media could be an effective tool, indeed a weapon" (Schiller).

In May, the Ramseys agreed to talk to a few reporters. There were strict limits imposed, and the media agreed. There would be no discussions about the murder, there would be lawyers present, but they could not be photographed with the Ramseys and they were not to be asked questions. No questions were allowed on the Ramseys' interaction with the police, the location of the interview was not to be disclosed, and the interview would only be thirty minutes long.

Of course, some in the media argued that this was unacceptable, but the story was too hot, and the terms were agreed on. Questions even arose about the Ramseys hiring public relations professionals. "In an industry where professionals are taught to tackle sensitive issues, how does one determine who would be a good client and who may be harmful to a firm's reputation?" (Vasquez, 1997).

Questioned about taking on clients who might be guilty, Russell said he believed there were no indications that his clients were guilty. With all the publicity, the district attorney began to wonder if the Ramseys would ever win in the public's mind. He wondered if he could get an impartial jury. The mainstream media had begun to take the same slant as the tabloids—that the Ramseys had killed their daughter. But the Ramseys were doing their own public relations campaigning. They had taken out advertisements, made up flyers, and sent direct mail. They had their advocates talk to the media. Mike Bynum, who was their close friend, was interviewed on ABC by Diane Sawyer and clearly stated he knew that the Ramseys were incapable of murder. This was clearly becoming a crime that was being tried in the media.

On October 2, 1997, the district attorney's press representative sent him a memo stating that they had been "beaten up" by the press and needed to restore their credibility. The memo stated that the best approach was to work the media before a formal statement was made and take no questions after. That was to be followed with a series of media appearances on the condition that he got an uninterrupted opportunity to speak.

It now seemed that everyone was putting conditions on the media, and the media was only too happy to agree. Would they, under any other circumstances, have compromised their ethics by agreeing to conditions under which interviews are conducted? It is doubtful, but this story had wide interest among the public, interest meant ratings, and ratings meant money. Are the facts in a case, the full and total story, able to compete with sponsors and profits? Does money enable this country to no longer have a truly free press?

In 1998, District Attorney Hunter continued his attack on the police department through the media. He said the police were so convinced that the Ramseys had committed the murder, they could not look at other evidence objectively. Although quoted in a national magazine as saying the police were inept, once the article was published, he said his comments were taken out of context.

In 1998, a grand jury was convened. Almost 80 members of the media were in attendance for the police department's presentation. There were live broadcasts and remote equipment from CNN, NBC, ABC, CBS, and Fox. In attendance as well were the tabloids, including the *National Enquirer* and *The Globe*, as well as *Extra*.

> We interviewed 590 people, consulted 64 outside experts, investigated and cleared more than 100 possible suspects, collected 1,058 pieces of evidence, tested over 500 items at federal, state and private laboratories, gathered handwriting and non-testimonial evidence. From 215 people, we built a case file that now bulged to 30,000 pages, reviewed more than 3,400 letters and 700 telephone tips and contacted seventeen states and two foreign countries. And it all kept leading us in one direction. The

detective team believed that John and Patsy Ramsey had knowledge of, and were involved in, the death of their daughter, JonBenet. (Thomas & Davis)

In August 1998, Steve Thomas resigned from the Boulder police, after sending a letter to Chief Beckner. He gave as his main reason for leaving the mishandling of the case by the district attorney's office. In that letter, he wrote, "Much of what appeared in the press was orchestrated by particular sources wishing to discredit the Boulder Police Department. We watched the media spin, while we were prohibited from exercising First Amendment rights" (Schiller).

According to Thomas, he sent three copies of the letter, one to a legal adviser, another to Commander Hayes, and one to Chief Becker. An hour later, he wrote, a reporter from *The Globe*, whom he had never met, showed up at his door with a copy of the letter. Thomas said the reporter had close contacts with the district attorney's office, and therefore felt that was where he had gotten the letter.

"By 5:30, my resignation was the top story on *ABC World News Tonight*. . . . For the rest of the night my telephone rang with calls from the media, which I didn't answer" (Thomas & Davis).

Reports were released stating that Thomas retired because of his health. Then, Thomas said, Jeff Shapiro, a reporter for *The Globe*, who had been following the case, first as an undercover assignment, told Thomas that the D.A.'s office was going to try to discredit him. He also said his own paper would be out after him.

Thomas then writes that *The Globe* wanted an interview with him, which he declined. He then received a package containing photos of his family. "It was the most revolting, sick and slimy thing I had ever encountered. The pictures were accompanied by a letter from Craig Lewis, saying he wanted to 'sit down and talk' . . . and help me with some background information, particularly the whole conflict between the cops and the district attorney. It was carefully worded, but the warning, pictures and letters were like some old Mafioso scheme, and to me it added up to extortion" (Thomas & Davis).

Thomas was concerned that they would slander his family and expose his mother's suicide. He had accused the paper as being the same one that the district attorney was "in bed with." Lewis denied any of the accusations, but, "in 1999, Craig Lewis was indicted in neighboring Jefferson County on charges of extortion and conspiracy for his work on the Ramsey stories and for his blatant attempt to force me to talk" (Thomas & Davis).

He said that it was only after the personal attacks against him, did Thomas say he decided to write a book. On October 13, 1999, Alex Hunter, the district attorney, called a press conference to announce that a grand jury that had begun deliberations thirteen months before had found insufficient evidence to charge any suspect in the killing of JonBenet.

In an attempt to tell their side of the story, John and Patsy signed a book deal with a publisher that specialized in religious books. The name of the book is *The Death of Innocence: The Untold Story of JonBenet's Murder and How Its Exploitation Compromised the Pursuit of Truth.*

Within days of that announcement, it was revealed that the Ramseys had hired L. Lin Wood, a prominent Atlanta libel attorney. Crimelibrary.com writes that he said of his defense: "People's eyes glaze over when you start talking about the First Amendment and privacy. But if we allow the media to try people outside of the judicial system, without any boundaries or limitations, everyone is at risk. Serious journalists need to start asking themselves: Do I want to be judge and jury for this person?"

The business aspect of public relations also entered into the controversy. "Today the buzz in corporate PR circles is to take the initiative, to bring the attack to the attacker. They call it 'hard ball.' The latest attorney the Ramseys hired to represent them, Lin Wood, believes very much in going on the offensive, of getting right in the face of the opposition" (*Time*, 1999).

On May 4, 2000, Greta Van Sustenen hosted *Larry King Live*. According to show's transcripts, Thomas criticized district attorney Alex Hunter, saying both his office and the police department shared the blame for the case not being solved. Ben Thompson, who was running for Hunter's seat, was also a guest. His promise to solve the case was attacked by guest Alan Dershowitz:

> This is the first time in my experience, thirty-six years in criminal law, I ever heard a man running for district attorney on the promise that he would arrest and presumably indict somebody. This would change the nature of our legal system. It would make it criminal justice by referendum. You would be voting for a person in order to get somebody indicted . . . this transcends the Ramsey case. I'm so worried, not so much about this case. I'm so worried about what's happening to American justice when you have a candidate running—he's running on the following basic claim. He says: Everybody all over America has seen television; they all know who did it. If you also . . . think you know who did it based on what you've seen on television, vote for me.

In January 2000, CBS began production of a miniseries based on the book, *Perfect Murder, Perfect Town*. The four-hour television movie aired February 27 and was followed by a statement by John Eller, who was, by then, the former Boulder police commander. In an interview in the *Rocky Mountain News,* he attacked the media coverage, calling it inaccurate, and said the books and movies would contaminate a future jury pool.

In March 2000, the Ramseys' book came out. The book also criticized the media and likened them to vultures that waited to find tidbits of flesh to pounce on. In April 2001, in their eighty-first update, the city of Boulder issued a press release in response to a television interview by Lou Smit: "In response to questions about Lou Smit and his Ramsey case theories, the Boulder Police Department believes it would be improper to debate the merits of the evidence in the public arena."

The book spurred a $50 million lawsuit by Chris Wolf against the Ramseys for libel. He was named in their book as one of the possible suspects. In what appeared to be an orchestrated offense, the Ramseys first challenged Thomas to face them on national television. He did, on CNN's *Larry King Live*.

Still on the offense, on August 31, 2000, *USA Today's* front-page headline read, "Patsy Ramsey issues challenge: If you think I did it, let's have a trial and get it over with."

In December 2003, the Ramseys, in another of a series of lawsuits they filed related to the murder, filed a $12 million federal defamation lawsuit in Atlanta against the Fox News Network. The story indicated that there was never any evidence to link an intruder to JonBenet's murder.

In 2004, John Ramsey announced his candidacy as a representative to the state's House of Representatives, stating that the tragedy and its aftermath inspired him to seek a way to contribute to society. He lost in a primary election in August.

Since the murder, at least sixteen books have been written. Schiller, in his beginning notes, says he wrote the book to attempt "to take the story of the murder investigation of JonBenet Ramsey out of the context of the newspapers reports and sound bites that have formed the nation's opinion of the case and place it into a more complete context" (Schiller).

His information was attacked by Steve Thomas, who says Schiller had been given access to his official police reports. He said he was "furious" and that "several witnesses called me to ask how their names and telephone numbers, which had been given to me in confidence, had ended up in the hands of an author. I went to see Commander Becker and protested the latest round of leaks from the district attorney's office, which was the only other place those reports were available. He later told me that Alex Hunter denied the accusation."

Thomas writes that Schiller later confirmed that his source was the district attorney's office, which had supplied him with fifteen hundred pages of police reports, memos, and other confidential information from the case file (Thomas & Davis).

Although the tragic murder of a young girl may never be solved, the case remains a study of the media's unrelenting need for information and the resulting manipulation, often orchestrated by public relations professionals. Would this case have been different if the Ramseys could not have afforded that kind of assistance? Would it have made national headlines if it did not occur at a "slow" news time, or if JonBenet had not been a beauty pageant winner?

Could this case have been solved if these factors did not exist? Unfortunately, we will never know. What we do know is the behavior of the media in this criminal investigation was a far cry from what one would consider careful investigation of a criminal case. If JonBenet had not been a beauty queen at the tender age of six years, would the media have cared?

## DISCUSSION QUESTIONS

1. How did the media's scrutiny affect the police investigations?
2. Should law enforcement be subject to this type of scrutiny and constant demands during murder investigations?
3. How much time should law enforcement spend answering to the media during an investigation?
4. Were the Ramseys wise in hiring public relations professionals to deal with the media?
5. Should the media have been so willing to allow the Ramseys to set the rules for interviews, and if so, why just for them?
6. How did this affect public opinion?
7. Does the fact that suspects have money and influence affect the way the media covers a crime? If so, how so?
8. Did politics and money play a role in this case?
9. Do you think that Steve Thomas was right in believing that the district attorney was able to spin the media coverage and the police department's investigation was hindered because of it? What implications does that have?

# 11

# Kobe Bryant, 2003

It was an alleged crime that is all too common in this country, a crime in which the victim is said to be victimized twice, once by the rapist and again by the court system. But in this case, the questions were different. Did the victim use the alleged rapist's celebrity status to get something for herself? Did the defendant's celebrity status put him in a position to be charged with rape? And did the social status of the accused help him get off?

It began on June 30, 2003, in a hotel near the famous Vail ski resort in Colorado. What both sides agreed on was that a young female hotel clerk voluntarily went into Kobe Bryant's room (the star Los Angeles Lakers basketball player), and that they flirted and kissed. Then the stories change. She told police officials he became violent, pushed her over a chair, and then raped her. He said the sex was consensual.

In July, he was charged with sexually assaulting the nineteen-year-old woman. He denied the charge and said he was only guilty of adultery.

He faced probation to life in prison if he was convicted on the single felony count. Bryant was freed on $25,000 bail, with the agreement that he would return to court in Eagle County on August 6, 2003, for a hearing.

What followed were months of closed-door hearings, numerous witnesses, and documents submitted and then redacted. The name of a woman who had previously accused Bryant of rape was blacked out on the documents.

Meanwhile, the court system continued to make almost unbelievable errors, including allowing confidential documents, to be released on its own Web site. Was this a usual occurrence that went unnoticed during less famous investigations, or was it intentional to feed the media's constant attention?

The judge in this case, in an attempt not to let the media overrun the judicial process, gave a severe warning to reporters that they would not get a seat in the courtroom if they published the name or photograph of the alleged victim. This resulted in a storm of controversy in the press, who argued that the ruling might be unconstitutional.

That ruling was only part of a three-page so-called "decorum order" by Eagle County Judge Frederick Gannett. The order outlined the ground rules for media that were planning to cover the upcoming August 6 hearing and future court appearances by Bryant.

A battle ensued between the media and the judge, with questions as to whether to release documents relating to the case. Judge Gannett said he saw it as a balancing act between the right to a fair trial and the public's right to know.

> Prosecutors urged Gannett to protect the victim from being "revictimized" by reports of her rape, and to prevent the media firestorm from getting hotter. According to prosecutor Gregg Crittendon, unsealing all the documents would "give the media all the ammunition it needed to conduct a full range, pretrial trial in the court of public opinion, tainting everyone from being possibly fair and impartial jurors in a trial." Coverage of Bryant's case, said the lawyer, isn't like news about Iraq or Afghanistan—it's "entertainment, tabloid news." (Bean, 2003)

In August, the judge officially rejected the media's request for detailed court records and agreed to unseal only the arrest warrant. He said the remaining documents would remained sealed until the case was finalized. The media was angered and claimed that the public was being short-changed.

In October 2003, Bryant was ordered to stand trial. Then, according to Foxnews.com, employees of the Eagle County sheriff's and district attorney's offices put in orders for a shipment of anti–Kobe Bryant T-shirts. Fox News reported they obtained a copy of the e-mail message ordering 76 shirts, which was allegedly written by the same sheriff's office that was investigating the case. On the front of the T-shirt was a hanging man. On the back was a choice of two derogatory statements about Bryant. Because of the publicity exposing the order Fox News reported, it was never completed.

Furniture from the hotel room where the alleged rape took place was auctioned off. The name of Bryant's alleged victim was posted on a message board on the Court TV Web site. Although only on the Web for a short time, it allowed the worldwide media, which was covering the story, to get important information. Earlier that year, another document was posted on the Colorado State Judicial Branch Web site that also included the accuser's name, and a transcript of a supposedly closed-door hearing was "accidentally" e-mailed to seven news organizations.

In what many considered a rare and unusual move, Judge W. Terry Ruckriegle, who was presiding over the trial, apologized for the clerical error. In July 2004, Judge Ruckriegle, in what became a controversial decision, ruled that extensive evidence about the sex life of the twenty-year-old woman seventy-two hours before the alleged rape could be given into evidence. This began a news media frenzy, with women's groups taking an even more prominent role in the case.

The alleged victim then let it be known she might not want to go to trial. The media began to reveal the factors that would contribute to making the trial a fair one.

> Color is one possible factor; class is another. There's a financial gulf between those who pay $175,000 for a golf-club membership and those who caddy for them. Most who work in Vail can't afford to live there. Trailer parks are home not just to carhops and maids but to social workers and the police. Could a local jury reflect the resentment the near poor have for the very rich? (Corliss, 2003)

And while the media hungrily waited for more developments, in August, two weeks before jury selection was to begin, lawyers for the woman filed a lawsuit in federal district court in Denver seeking monetary damages. Media outlets quickly began questioning her motives and credibility.

In August, Kobe Bryant's attorneys began questioning jury candidates behind closed doors after Judge Ruckriegle rejected a request to let the media listen in. The judge also rejected a request by the alleged victim to no longer place court documents online after her name and other details were mistakenly released. The judge said that while he regretted the mistakes, going back to paper documentation would have a minimal impact. On August 12, 2004, prosecutors asked for a delay in the trial, saying they would have problems getting an unbiased jury. Two days later, their request was denied.

In the lead story in the national report in the *New York Times*, the alleged crime took on another perspective.

> As recently as a generation ago, the fact that Kobe Bryant is black and the woman who has accused him of rape is white would probably have been enough to reawaken at least a few of the ghosts that rattle around America's attic. Many men have been lynched on the basis of lesser

accusations. But as the first prospective jurors file in for questioning here on Friday for the beginning of Mr. Bryant's sexual-assault trial, and nearly 600 journalists from around the world descend to record every twitch, many of the totems and taboos that might have once framed and defined the case were conspicuously absent. Some scholars and social critics say the simple answer was that society has traded one set of preoccupations for another. Race, as an issue of trial strategy and social debate, had been supplanted in the Bryant case and by questions of celebrity and class: What really separated the defendant from an accuser was not color but power. Mr. Bryant had the power in abundance as a wealthy basketball star for the Los Angeles Lakers and his accuser, a former front desk clerk at a hotel from a small town in Colorado, did not. (Johnson, 2004, p. A12)

The article goes on to reveal other consequences of the media attention on the trail: "The trial . . . also revealed much about how Colorado's rape victim protection law works, or does not, under the glare of a celebrity case. The law, like many others around the country, is meant to prevent defense lawyers from attacking an accuser's character by presenting evidence about her sex life" (Johnson).

Does it take media attention on a high-profile case to reveal or defend laws? Are there no other checks and balances in our system?

In the end, it was not clear who won. On September 1, 2004, the rape case against Kobe Bryant was dropped. Prosecutors said the woman who had accused him of sexual assault was unwilling to testify, leaving the state no option but to drop all charges against him.

Mr. Bryant issued a statement apologizing for his behavior and saying that while he believed the behavior was consensual, he could understand why she did not view it in the same way. He walked out a free man, but he was by no account a complete winner. He lost endorsement deals with McDonald's and Nutella, although he did keep his popularity among fans.

It may have cost his accuser more. William Scank, a potential juror and resident of Eagle, said, "Whether she was right or wrong, she can't show her face around here. . . . Kobe, I don't think it hurt him at all. He came out smelling like a rose" (*New York Times*, 2004, p. A14) .

The story went on to quote a Los Angeles film producer, twenty-two-year-old Elyse Sara; "It's very rare that celebrities end up serving a harsh prison sentence. . . . I'm not surprised it ended like this."

*Newsday* gave the story front-page coverage with a picture of Bryant and "Case Dismissed" as its headline. In a small section in the corner of the front page was a picture of the back of his accuser. The lead story explained the details:

A media maelstrom and courtroom chaos was quashed before it began with the case becoming even weaker. . . . The Kobe Bryant case was forever poised to become a media maelstrom: a basketball superstar from Los Angeles with a squeaky clean image accused of rape by a small-town woman, who, it was soon reported, had a history of emotional problems. (Kass, 2004, p. A4).

The small town of Eagle, Colorado, had seen the effects of a media hurricane. "For the past year, residents of this small town h[ad] watched as hordes of journalists descended, armed with cameras, notebooks and endless questions about what made the place tick" (Kelly, 2004, p. A12).

The people in the town of Eagle were described as relieved that the media has left. "For Eagle, a town of 4,500 that was invaded by up to 400 journalists every time Mr. Bryant made a court appearance, the sense of relief was evident" (Madigan & Sink, 2004, p. A14).

In October 2004, a federal judge denied a request from the alleged victim to remain anonymous in her civil lawsuit. He ruled that the public's interest in open court proceedings outweighed her desire to shield her identity.

Should the case have been brought to trial in the first place? The media was quick to take on that question as well. Would this case have ever been taken in the first place if it did not involve a famous athlete? "From the beginning, Eagle County, Colorado, District Attorney Mark Hurlbert insisted that the sexual-assault charge he filed against Kobe Bryant had nothing to do with the celebrity of the Los Angeles Lakers' star. But from the beginning, legal experts wondered whether a Rocky Mountain lawman would have filed such a case had the defendant been anything other than Hollywood-famous" (Saporito, 2004).

What role did the media play in this? Dahlia Lithwick, a guest columnist for the *New York Times* in August 2004, wrote, "With his right to a fair trial and her right to be spared a second assault on a collision course, the role of the media becomes absolutely lethal. In the Bryant case, by insisting on its constitutional right to act as watchdog, the press gained access to the most lurid details of the accuser's intimate life. Consequently, high-profile rape trials allow the media to do far more damage than rape shield laws ever tried to mitigate." When the national media exposes a woman's sexual history, it means the difference between shaming her in her community and doing so worldwide (Lithwick, 2004, sec. 4, p. 11).

Other media also weighed in. "But it is not a conviction or even a verdict, and Bryant's accuser may be saddled with a kind of fame she never bargained for. 'It has ruined the life that she's known,' said

Strickland of his ex-girlfriend. 'Her future is pretty well set for her. She's not allowed to put it behind her' " (Saporito, 2004).

As the publicity surrounding the case increased, the accuser became a victim, whether for the first or the second time. "The case collapsed last week after Bryant's accuser, the target of death threats and harassment since she was accidentally outed by the court, declined to testify against him. And in what seemed to be a programmed *pas de deux* settling the civil case she also filed against him, Bryant apologized to her, saying, 'I now understand how she sincerely feels that she did not consent to this encounter' " (Saporito, 2004).

The press's impact on a celebrity's reputation was obvious.

> For Mr. Bryant's part, it's not surprising that when the traditional defenses in a he says/she says case became unavailable to him in court, those same defenses were trotted out for the national press. As far as Mr. Bryant and his counsel are concerned, from the moment the district attorney peered into the flashbulbs and labeled him a rapist, his life was over, whether he was convicted or acquitted. You just don't meet a lot of babies named O.J. anymore. And so Mr. Bryant found in the media an eager handmaid to help him around the rape shield problem, clearing him through leaks, insinuations and repeated use of his accuser's name. In that one sense, rape law is not unlike campaign finance reform law—block one path and the sludge just oozes elsewhere. (Lithwick, 2004, sec. 4, p. 11)

What was accomplished by the onslaught of media hype? It appears little more was gained than the right of the media to pick the cases they want to cover, and cover them in the way they want.

> Another star athlete charged with sexual malice? Such an item is usually confined to that burgeoning beat, the sports-page police blotter. Kobe Bryant makes it front-page news—not simply because he and Shaquille O'Neal are the Guts and Godzilla of the star-studded Lakers, not because he scored 30 points a game last season or because he went straight from high school legend to NBA phenomenon. Not even because he recently inked a $45 million endorsement deal with Nike. But because he is one of the NBA's prime icons of clean and keen. (Corliss, 2003)

Of course, although all of this happened in a relatively short time span and there was no trial, there had to be a book. It was not a great seller. It was written by a tabloid reporter named Jeffery Scott Shapiro and called, *Kobe Bryant: The Game of His Life*. The book, only 160 pages long, was supposed to be handed out on the steps of the courtroom. It never made it there. Shapiro wound up selling rights to the book to the *New York Daily News*.

The Web site thesmokinggun.com has the full transcript of Bryant's interview with the police in July 2003.

The media was all over this story, which can only lead to the question: Was that coverage valid?

> But it's not the first time TV news shows have tackled juicy stories with saturation coverage, whether it's the latest celebrity trial (Michael Jackson, Martha Stewart, Kobe Bryant, etc.) or a lurid missing person case. Are they news? To an extent, they are when big-name celebrities or local residents are involved. But 24-hour coverage, with rampant and often irresponsible guesswork to fill time when nothing new is learned, is way over the top. (Gainsvilletimes.com, 2005)

Attorney Andrew Cohen, a legal analyst for CBS News and CBS news.com, wrote on July 30, 2004, about the case,

> It makes me wish I could ship the whole cast to some island and make them fight it out amongst themselves in private so that the rest of us don't have to be brought along for the nasty, ugly ride. And I haven't felt that emotion since the high of the Ramsey investigation, when the police were fighting with prosecutors and the Ramseys were fighting with the media and no one seemed to be focusing upon the poor little girl who had brought them all together. Whatever happened inside that hotel room last June 30th between Bryant and his alleged victim is a tragedy on some level; surely everyone involved can and should do better in reacting to it and dealing with it.

And after all the publicity and last-minute headlines, Mr. Cohen wrote, "That's happening now, as a zany week comes to end in a case that would seem silly if it weren't just so sad."

But would it have been all of this if the accused were a celebrity? Would there have been a crime at all? Sadly, all indications are the answer would be no.

## DISCUSSION QUESTIONS

1. Did the steady stream of court errors occur because the case was in the media spotlight, or because it took place in the American court system?

2. Should the exposing of those errors have caused an investigation into the court system?

3. If the media hadn't benefited from the results, would they have called for an investigation?

4. Why didn't the media spend more time on the faults in the system as opposed to the chain of events that led to the accusations?

5. Would the alleged victim have gone to trial if the case were not as public?

6. Was she victimized by the press?

7. Should there be more safeguards for alleged victims of rape to protect them in these types of cases? Or should there be more safeguards for those being accused who are in the public eye?

8. Does being a celebrity in today's society make you more vulnerable because the media is quicker to pick up on an alleged crime?

9. Why do think race was not brought into this trial as it was in the case of O.J. Simpson?

# 12

# Daniel Pelosi, 2001

A wealthy man found dead in his house. Under normal circumstances (if there can be normal circumstances in media coverage), the story would run for a few days, and then perhaps there would be some coverage of the trial. But, if the media finds things in the story that they think might sell, the story can stay alive for years, and in the case of Daniel Pelosi, it did just that.

The victim was tall, dark, and handsome. He led the lifestyle of the rich and famous. He had just about everything going for him. But he had one major problem. Someone wanted to kill him and eventually that person succeeded.

That is just the beginning of a tale that kept the media's attention for months. The murder, which took place in one of the nation's playgrounds for the wealthy, quickly became a media feast filled with money, sex, status, and intrigue.

The story began on October 21, 2001, when a wealthy New York City financier, Theodore Ammon, was found beaten to death in his East Hampton estate in Long Island, New York. Investigators did not take long to focus on Daniel Pelosi, an electrician who was having an affair with Ammon's wife, Generosa. The couple met while Pelosi was doing work in the Ammons' Upper East Side, New York City townhouse. Pelosi, described as a hustler with an oversized bravado, waited in his truck for days to meet with Generosa, while he left his wife and children at home. Unemployed, he needed the job of renovating her townhouse. He got both the job and the girl. Soon after they met, he left his wife and three children and moved into a hotel in Manhattan, where Generosa was also living. During the summer of

2000, Generosa had filed for divorce and was looking for more than $1 million a year in living expenses.

In the fall of 2000, she hired Pelosi. Before long, they started dating and the following summer, Pelosi started hanging out in the Hamptons with her. On October 22, 2001, Ammon's body was discovered. After Ammon's death, Pelosi and Generosa both hired the same attorney. Only three months later, on January 10, 2002, Generosa and Pelosi were married. Their hasty marriage did little for their relationship, which quickly became stressed.

Pelosi liked partying, drinking, and, by many accounts, doing drugs. After Generosa was diagnosed with cancer, Kathryn Mayne, her nanny, became a central character in her life. She and Pelosi constantly argued. Reports say Mayne told her employer that her new husband was cheating on her and spending all her money.

On August 22, 2003, Generosa died of breast cancer, and the following month, Pelosi sought to get out of his $2 million postnuptial agreement that denied him the right to contest her will. Ted Ammon had left Generosa $80 million. She left the bulk of her estate to her children.

Pelosi's strange behavior was reported by the press:

> When Long Island contractor Danny Pelosi, 40, brought the ashes of his dead, estranged wife Generosa Ammon with him to the bar at Manhattan's swank Stanhope Hotel last week, it was only the latest bizarre installment in the titillating tale of the fall of the house of Ammon. So far, the story involves the unsolved murder of a dashing multimillionaire at his East Hampton, NY, estate, a felonious electrician, a missing laptop, a handsomely compensated British nanny, and now a dispute over a dead woman's remains. "If this was on *Dallas*, nobody would believe it," said Steven Gaines, author of *Philistines at the Hedgerow: Passion and Property in the Hamptons*. "It's amazing. It's horrible." (Winters, 2003)

On March 22, 2004, a Suffolk County jury indicted Pelosi on second-degree murder, after it had reportedly questioned 51 witnesses. The next day, Pelosi pleaded not guilty. In April 2004, a trial date of September 1, 2004, was set and on September 24, a pool of jurors chosen from over 500 in a three-week period was in place.

What made this story so important to the media? One of the many reasons was the location. East Hampton is a small village on the South Shore of Long Island and is known as one of the leading playgrounds for the rich and famous. The Ammon murder was only the second murder in that village since it was incorporated in 1920. Although it has its own police department, the county's homicide detectives would investigate the case. A lieutenant in the East Hampton police department was reported to have said he knew the case was going to attract major attention and he did not want his department to look inept after what transpired in Colorado with the JonBenet Ramsey case. With Suffolk County handling the investigation, his department would be off the hook, and the problems of an investigation would be handled by a department that had more resources.

There would be a massive amount of media interest in the case, and his decision later proved to be a wise one. The media pounced on the story and did not let go until years later when the trial was over.

The investigation would prove to be a difficult one—there was no apparent murder weapon, no witnesses, and little evidence. The media could not get enough of it. It seemed as if every day there were new media-rich developments. The background of the case was what books are made of, and later, of course, were.

An ugly divorce . . . a widow with a large estate. She quickly marries her lover and moves out of the country to England. They return after she is diagnosed with breast cancer, and weeks before her death they split up. She changes her will and gives most of the estate to her adopted twin children. What was left after her death, her estranged husband spends on liquor and gambling. Her ex-husband is found murdered and her husband is indicted and is charged with second-degree murder. He is ordered to await trial in prison. What better plot for a suspense story?

It was the media's idea of a dream story. Events kept the story constantly in the news, making it more like a soap opera than a murder investigation. The public's eyes were fixed on this story.

Pelosi's past and his relationship with Generosa became the immediate focus of the media. When Generosa died, Pelosi was left as the only suspect. The media once again pounced on the new aspects of this ongoing story. Meanwhile, Ammon's bank, as co-executor of the estate, filed a wrongful death suit against Pelosi.

During this time, Pelosi served four months in jail for a drunk driving conviction in 2003. The media even printed a letter he wrote to his father from jail: "Desperate and lonely, Daniel Pelosi wrote a letter to his father from jail, begging to stop their feud. 'I'm sorry and I love you,' he wrote in April 2003, while serving time for drunk driving. 'I do not want to carry the cross of pain in never hearing your voice again.' The letter was later used as evidence in his trial" (Bruchey, 2003).

When the actual murder case began in 2004, the media made it a daily ritual to be there. The prosecutor, Suffolk County Assistant

District Attorney Janet Albertson, was described as a down-to-earth, hard-hitting, no-nonsense attorney. The defendant's attorney was considered high profile and the best that money could buy.

Albertson, unlike many attorneys who take part in high-profile cases, was not interested in the publicity. She was protective of her family and declined many interviews. At the age of forty-three, she had gained a reputation of being one of the most respected prosecutors in the region.

The head of the defense team, Gerald Shargel, was known to represent alleged mobsters, and more specifically, had gotten a surprise acquittal for mob boss John Gotti in 1990 from charges he had ordered a hit on a union official. He made it a point to play to the media. At sixty, he was known to take on mostly high-profile cases and to enjoy the resulting publicity.

But it was Albertson who brought the first sensationalism to the courtroom. On September 29, 2004, the first day of the trial, before the jury was brought in and in front of a packed courtroom, she announced that she had taped recordings of Mr. Pelosi that proved he was making plans to intimidate and harm witnesses, tamper with his jury, and threaten her children. The recordings had been made in prison.

A decision would have to be made on the admissibility of the tapes, but Mr. Shargel, in a sudden display of anger, accused the prosecution of staging the last-minute revelation of the tapes and said he could no longer get a fair trial. The case was adjourned until October 3, 2004.

On October 12, 2004, Pelosi was arraigned on new charges. This time it was a sixteen-count indictment that included attempted assault of witnesses, attempted jury tampering, criminal solicitation, and conspiracy. With all the media attention, the judge in the case was forced to interview jurors the next day to see if they were still able to be impartial.

While the national media continued to cover the story, the *New York Times* reported that even the local residents were losing interest:

> The third anniversary of R. Theodore Ammon's death passed like any other day in East Hampton in the fall, a season when residents are returning to the routine of small-town life after the busy summer. The details of how Mr. Ammon, a Manhattan venture capitalist, was beaten to death at his summer home here have finally begun to unfold in a Riverhead courtroom 30 miles away, attracting the attention of the national media and generating headlines in the daily papers. But here in East Hampton, the talk of the town isn't the killing, the secret

surveillance system in Mr. Ammon's mansion, or Mr. Ammon's embittered wife and her blue-collar lover, who is now charged with the crime. Instead, bartenders, cashiers, and waitresses up and down Montauk Highway offered a collective shrug when asked about the level of interest in the case on the East End. (Beller, 2004)

So, if the locals weren't interested, why did the press want to keep the story alive? They still saw a sexy story and were not ready to let go.

In August 2004, State Supreme Court Justice Robert Doyle ruled that a laptop computer was used by Pelosi's sister to remotely turn off the security system in the Ammons' house on the weekend he was murdered. When the trial resumed, it did not take long before another twist brought more media attention.

The *New York Times* reported that there were two trials going on at the same time:

The official one was for Daniel J. Pelosi, a Long Island electrician charged with murdering the Manhattan financier, R. Theodore Ammon. But, as Mr. Pelosi's defense delivered its opening statement, it became clear that Mr. Ammon's sexuality would also be on trial. The prosecutor, Janet Albertson, argued before a jury in State Supreme Court here that Mr. Pelosi's motive was simple—he committed murder to get rich. She said he first wooed Mr. Ammon's estranged wife in 2000 and then killed him in October 2001 to get at his $80 million fortune. Mr. Pelosi's lawyer, Gerald Shargel, laid out another scenario to explain the murder. He suggested Mr. Ammon had led a hidden double life that ended when a gay lover beat him to death as he lay in bed in his East Hampton mansion, then stole Mr. Ammon's underwear and sheets to cover his tracks. Mr. Shargel said a mysterious hair and a spot of blood substantiated his claim. (Healy, 2004).

What more could the media want for good daily stories? Now the idea of sexuality brought another angle. Each twist and turn of the trial gave them more material for sensational daily updates.

Kathryn Ann Mayne, the nanny for the Ammon children, testified that Pelosi told her on two occasions that he had murdered Mr. Ammon. Pelosi's ex-girlfriend, Tracey Riebenfeld, also testified he admitted his guilt, saying he had a monster inside him. A former inmate said he also was told by Pelosi that he killed Ammon, but he was not called to testify. Two other individuals also said Pelosi confessed to them.

As the trial continued with its bizarre occurrences, perhaps the strangest of all happened in the beginning of November 2004. What better way to bring on more media coverage than to bring in the occult? "The themes of sex, avarice, and revenge that have coursed through the murder trial of Daniel Pelosi suddenly seem pedestrian. In an outlandish moment that brought the trial to an immediate halt yesterday afternoon, Pelosi's lawyer told a judge in Riverhead that his client's family believed Pelosi's wife, Generosa Ammon, was the devil and that she had cast a spell on their entire family" (Bruchey & Topping, 2004).

One of Pelosi's sisters blamed Generosa for the death of her brother. "The allegations of magic spells and curses set off a flurry of legal parrying that State Supreme Court Justice Robert W. Doyle said he would resolve after seeing legal briefs from both sides" (Bruchey & Topping, 2004).

The jury was excused for the day, and even the *New York Times* picked up on this strange turn of events. "The murder case against Daniel Pelosi . . . was already plenty bizarre with tales of $300,000 hotel bills, secret surveillance systems and stolen human ashes. But on Thursday, it entered the realm of the occult" (Healy, 2004).

The Pelosis said they believed Generosa was a witch, saying they saw the face of a demon appear in a photo of Pelosi's dead brother. They also said they saw her shoes beside a tree in a family member's backyard. "The spell stuff starts as soon as the brother dies," Mr. Shargel said outside the court. "The devil enters when she sees the shoes."

The trial took eight weeks. Closing arguments ended on December 11, 2004. The media covered every day and every new development. Two days later there was a verdict. Pelosi was found guilty of second-degree murder. In the end, there was speculation that it was his own testimony that made the case against him.

On December 14, 2004, *Newsday* had a front-page headline that read, "Pelosi Guilty, It Was His Big Mouth. Jurors, prosecutor say electrician's testimony helped convict him of millionaire's murder."

The *New York Times* placed as their lead story in the Metro section: "Pelosi guilty of murder of lover's husband in Hamptons." Patrick Healy reported that "the verdict caps one of Long Island's most-watched criminal cases in years, a three-year murder mystery laced with stories of betrayal, adultery, greed, and stun guns" (Healy, 2004).

But it was not be over for Pelosi. He faced twenty-five years to life in prison. At that time, he also faced charges of trying to intimidate witnesses and tamper with the jury. In an unrelated case, Pelosi was charged with stealing $43,000 of electricity from the local electric company. He also faced charges of an assault in Hawaii, where he allegedly punched a crew member during a dinner cruise.

But, as much as the media devoured every new angle of the case for years, they were just as quick to lose interest. On December 17, 2004, Pelosi was back at the courthouse minus most of the press and his high-powered lawyers. His lawyers explained their absence by saying they didn't know he was having a conference on the jury tampering and intimidating witness charges.

The story continued when on April 6, 2005, *Newsday* reported that Pelosi was back in court to face the last of his criminal charges. A plea deal based on his sixteen-count indictment had been arranged that would add three years to his twenty-five years to life sentence. But, at the last minute, Pelosi backed out.

District Attorney Thomas Spota was reported as saying, "It's his mouth that is always his downfall. We were giving him a break . . . this man just doesn't get it." He added that if Pelosi were now convicted in a trial, he would get an additional fifteen years in prison.

The media loved the story. The *Daily News* led with "Convicted killer Danny Pelosi just doesn't know when to shut his trap. The Long Island Lothario lost a cushy plea deal yesterday by doing what he does best—opening his big mouth" (Williams, 2005).

The *New York Post* reported, "Convicted murderer Danny Pelosi's big mouth has gotten him into trouble again—this time sinking a plea bargain that would have gotten him only three years in jail, instead of 15 if convicted. . . . Pelosi later told *the Post* from jail: 'I was up all night and totally confused. There were too many questions. I didn't understand the charge' " (Crowley, 2005).

Three years after Theodore Ammon's death, the *New York Times* confirmed that interest in the case had waned. It appeared that the story had no new angles, no more twists and turns, nothing to entice a new surge of interest. "Three months earlier, the publicist Lizzie Grubman had backed her SUV over 16 bystanders outside a Southampton nightclub after calling a bouncer there 'white trash,' touching off a media blitz in the Hamptons. . . . In contrast with the Pelosi trial, residents seemed to take a more personal interest in the Grubman case, probably because she had incurred their anger by her comment" (Beller, 2004).

Every aspect of this case had been dissected by the media. The lives of all the key players were replayed from their childhood over and over again. But some believe the story will always remain alive.

In a three-full-page story in *Newsday*, Samuel Bruchey quoted tabloid journalism professor Suzanne Ely as saying, "However this saga plays out in court . . . the tabloids will be following these kids. When they're 18 and have all that money, but still living with the tragedy, what will become of them? It's a story that sells" (Bruchey, 2004).

In May 2005, the end seemed near, or was it? Pelosi copped a plea.

"Pelosi told Justice Robert Doyle to ignore everything he has said, in a long, rambling statement in court last month—when he derailed his plea bargain by shooting off his mouth. He then stifled himself and pleaded guilty to attempted witness tampering while he was being tried for killing multimillionaire Ted Ammon" (Crowley, May 5, 2005).

It was good day for the media to pick up the story. "Daniel Pelosi finally figured out how to plead guilty yesterday," reported *Newsday* (Dowdy, 2005, p. A22).

Maybe the media would figure out how to let the story go. But perhaps that is the key to covering sensational trials. How long do they sell? This story may never really be over. Many media outlets have already expressed interest in the children and what will happen to them. Tune in for the next chapter in the Ammon murder saga.

## DISCUSSION QUESTIONS

1. What made this coverage of a murder different from the thousands that happen every year in this country?
2. Would the media have shown so much attention if the Ammons were not as wealthy as they were?
3. Why was Ted Ammon's sexuality so important to the media?
4. Did Daniel Pelosi's personality play a part in the amount of media coverage of the trial? And if so, how?
5. Is there ever overcoverage by the media? For example, what effect will it have/or did it have on the Ammons' children?

# 13

# Elizabeth Ann Smart, 2002

Thousands of children, unfortunately, go missing every year. What is even more disturbing is that only a handful actually get media attention. The story of Elizabeth Ann Smart is a case study of a kidnapping that captured the media's attention, but it is also a study of why one case can go virtually unnoticed and another take up daily headlines.

Why do the media choose to focus on one child, yet ignore others? What made Elizabeth's story different? This case is important in that it not only highlights how the media covered the disappearance of Elizabeth, but it also leads to questions on why they choose not to highlight other missing children. Elizabeth might never have been found had it not been for the media coverage, and so, one must ask, do the media no longer report the news, but have become an essential part of it?

Sometimes, the media is not just the all-consuming monster that preys on the voyeuristic weaknesses of the general public. Sometimes, it can actually help in solving a crime. It is at those rare times that the similarities between law enforcement and the media become even more apparent.

The case in point: the kidnapping of fourteen-year-old Elizabeth Ann Smart. Elizabeth was kidnapped from her bedroom in her family's 6,600-square-foot home in Salt Lake City, Utah, on June 5, 2002. Her parents and four brothers were asleep, but her nine-year-old sister, who shared the same bedroom, only pretended to be asleep. She waited two hours before getting out of her bed to tell her parents, Ed and Lois Smart, that Elizabeth had been kidnapped.

The case immediately captured national media attention. Police in Salt Lake City focused their investigation on a man they already had in custody for an unrelated crime. The suspect, Richard Ricci, later died from a brain hemorrhage while in prison. The Laura Recovery Center organized a massive search for Elizabeth. The search lasted for a week before it was called off, and volunteers were urged to find other ways to find Elizabeth. Volunteers had searched through the city and mountain foothills, but it was difficult to keep up the momentum. On the first day of the search, according to the Associated Press, 1,200 people volunteered; six days later the number had dwindled to 200. The search did expand into other areas. One of Elizabeth's uncles, Tom Smart, asked for approximately fifty all-terrain-vehicle owners to help search the West Desert area of Utah. A spokesman for the family said that fifty-five owners showed up, each searching a twenty-five-square-mile area.

On June 11, 2002, according to the Associated Press, Chief Rick Dinse, head of the city's police department, told reporters that the investigators were going to refocus their investigation. Using the media as a tool to talk with her abductors, Chief Dinse said, "We are going to get you. If you've got Elizabeth, you better release her now." He further elaborated by stating, "We believe that is possible that we have already talked to, or will soon talk to, the suspect that is responsible for this crime. My caution to this suspect, if he is listening, is 'we are going to get you.' "

The media had become an ally of the police department, each using the other for their own purposes. Four months later, Mary Katherine, Elizabeth's younger sister, said she thought she might know who the abductor was. She identified him as a person the family knew and who had done work on their house for a day.

In February, police released a description of the man, but did not supply a name or a photograph. That man was arrested under a false name more than a week later in San Diego, California. He was not recognized by police and was released.

The Smarts, not knowing of the arrest, but needing to keep the media interested and updated on the story, were getting more and more frustrated and more media savvy. They persistently tried to keep the story alive in the media, hoping the more exposure they got, the better the chances of finding their daughter. The media was more than happy to oblige. The Smarts gave the media home movies and put over twenty photos of Elizabeth on a Web site. These photos were downloaded for both the media and pamphlets.

With the massive attention, talk shows began their own speculation. Commentators such as Larry King shared their thoughts with the public. The Smarts went as far as accusing the police of not doing their job. Eventually, Mary Katherine's description did lead to a sketch that was broadcast and distributed nationally. The sketch was recognized by the accused's family members, who then supplied authorities with actual pictures.

Elizabeth's disappearance was the first time the state of Utah used its Emergency Alert System, the Rachel Alert. It had been created only months before to quickly broadcast information about an abducted child. Within four hours of the local police being notified of Elizabeth's disappearance, the alert went into effect.

The Rachel Alert in Utah was named after a young girl who was abducted and killed in 1982. It was adapted from the Amber plan, which was named for nine-year-old Amber Hagerman, who was abducted and murdered in Texas in 1996. At the time of Elizabeth's disappearance, Utah was only the ninth state in the country to establish the program.

The alerts are an example of the best type of cooperation between law enforcement and the media. As the alerts are put out, there are not only signs along the highways, but local media outlets broadcast the details as well. With the media working with law enforcement, the chances for recovery greatly increase. The media certainly helped in solving Elizabeth's kidnapping.

Brian David Mitchell, who had worked at the Smart residence as a handyman, was now officially wanted by police for questioning. Mitchell, forty-nine, was a drifter and a self-described prophet who called himself Emmanuel. His traveling companion and alleged wife was named Wanda Eileen Barzee.

A little over eight months after Elizabeth's abduction, a tip came to police that a man resembling Mitchell was seen walking down a street accompanied by two females in the Salt Lake City suburb of Sandy. According to CNN.com,

> Witness John Ferguson described an older couple "calmly talking to police." But Sandy Police Chief Steve Chapman said when police officers confronted the couple, "they were evasive in some of their answers." After further questioning, police were certain the man was Mitchell and the girl Elizabeth. At the time, she was wearing a wig, sunglasses, a blue overcoat and something resembling a veil.

CNN.com went on to quote one of the callers who tipped police off as saying, "I don't really feel like I've done any great thing. I did not think about any reward. I'm a mother with seven children."

After Elizabeth was identified as being safe, other people came forward with stories of sightings of her, saying she did not seem to be held against her will. According to Answers.com,

She was even photographed attending a party wearing a veil and on another occasion, strolling with Mitchell and Barzee in a park. Peer–peer networks had ostensibly been circulating a video of Smart freely roaming about during parties she attended. Other attendees of those parties were not aware that Smart was a kidnapping victim and Smart did not attempt to seek their help. There is speculation that Smart may have been a willing participant rather than a helpless victim. In response, the Smart family claims that Elizabeth willingly cooperated only because she was brainwashed by Mitchell and Barzee into believing that God wanted her to be Mitchell's wife.

The media could now focus on another angle of the story: the lurid details of Elizabeth's captivity. But, according to Colin Allen in an article in *Psychology Today* written on Psychologytoday.com,

> One can only guess what psychological trauma Elizabeth Smart has endured. The abducted teen from Salt Lake City returned home last week after nine months in captivity. Her family says she was perhaps brainwashed by the homeless couple that abducted her, Brian Mitchell and Wanda Barzee. Even when police questioned her in Salt Lake City last Wednesday, she said she was Mitchell's daughter.

As with most high-profile cases, there has to be media controversy on almost every aspect of the crime. In Allen's article, he said,

> Myrna Shure, professor at Drexel University in Philadelphia, Pennsylvania, doesn't believe Smart was brainwashed. "If she were truly brainwashed, she would not want to see her family. On the contrary she may be suffering from Stockholm syndrome, in which the abductee becomes emotionally attached to her captors. We don't know whether she has genuinely bonded with them," Shure states.

On the Psychology Today Web site, other professionals weighed in on the subject. Adolph W. Cwik, MA, from Boyne City, Michigan, recommended that the entire family be removed from all publicity. Elisabeth Wassenaar, from Monterey, California, wrote, "Going any deeper into speculation would be journalistic sensationalism. It may make good reading for the layman, but [it] would have no more clinical validity than the speculations we hear in the media about the war on Iraq." (Allen, March 18, 2003). But none of that would stop the press from keeping the story alive.

The media had its main feature and would not let go. It lavished its attention on the moments before the police knew it was Elizabeth and had approached her on the street. Almost every media outlet had detailed descriptions of the events and played them over and over.

According to a March 14, 2003, Associated Press report,

> When officers approached the teen, Officer Bill O'Neal said, "She kind of just blurted out, 'I know who you think I am. You guys think I'm that Elizabeth Smart girl who ran away.'" Smart told police her name was Augustine and that her cheap black sunglasses protected her eyes while they healed from surgery. When they asked why she wore a wig and T-shirt for a head scarf, she became upset. "Her heart was beating so hard you could see it through her chest," O'Neal said. Handcuffed and loaded into a separate police car from Mitchell and Barzee for the ride to the station, Smart began to cry. "We kept telling her, do this for your family, do this for yourself. Do the right thing—we know you're Elizabeth Smart," said Sergeant Victor Quezada. Smart responded with a biblical quote, "Thou sayest."

The report went on to describe Elizabeth's first night with her family, who said she appeared to adjust well.

> Sierra Smart said she and several other cousins spent about three hours with Elizabeth. "She's like totally talking, totally casual," said Sierra, 22. "She got all new clothes. She gave a fashion show." Elizabeth may have been kept from escaping or crying out for help by the growing influence of her captors, police said. Investigators have not talked to her since Wednesday evening and have no immediate plans to interview her again, Dinse said.

Even after exposing every detail about Elizabeth being found, the media hype was not about to end. In the first five days after Elizabeth returned home, the family spokesman received more than 3,000 media calls and nearly 100 film, book, or made-for-TV movie proposals. In the first hours after she was found, more than three million people went to the Web site created for Elizabeth.

In the midst of all this, the *Salt Lake Tribune* fired two reporters who were reportedly paid $20,000 for collaborating with the *National Enquirer* on the Elizabeth Smart story. They allegedly misled their editors as to their involvement in the story.

According to the Associated Press, *Tribune* editor James E. Shelledy "said Monday that Vigh and Cantera split $20,000 for their help on a July 2 *Enquirer* story headlines 'Utah Cops: Secret Diary Exposes Family Sex Ring.' The story has been retracted as part of a settlement between the Smart family and the tabloid." Soon after that, Shelledy resigned.

On the positive side, where there is mass publicity, there is politics, and once again the issue found its way to the White House. President Bush signed a child protection bill that encouraged states to set up Amber Alert systems to find abducted children.

In January 2005, Elizabeth Smart's school records were subpoenaed by Mitchell's attorneys. Her father had asked that a plea agreement be reached to keep Elizabeth from being put on the witness stand.

Of course, there had to be books. After Elizabeth was home, her family published a book, *Bringing Elizabeth Home*, which was also used as the basis of a television movie that aired in November 2003. According to Answers.com, "The Smarts claimed they wanted to avoid subjecting their daughter to the limelight, but that after realizing it was inevitable, they decided it would be preferable to be involved in the process and offered input during the making of the movie."

But Elizabeth's immediate family could not keep their own rights to future books. A little over two years after her safe return, her uncle, Tom Smart, coauthored a controversial book entitled, *In Plain Sight: The Startling Truth Behind the Elizabeth Smart Investigation*. According to the Associated Press, he blasted the police in the book.

> Smart's uncle has faulted the police investigation into her disappearance in a new book, claiming the teen would still be a kidnap victim if the family had not gotten involved. "I don't think she would be back," Tom Smart said. "There's five or six things that had to happen and all those things, thank God, happened, including help from the community, which raised awareness to find Elizabeth." While grateful for the "tireless efforts" of law enforcement, Tom Smart and coauthor Lee Benson claim that in August 2002, two months after Elizabeth disappeared, police were alerted by a caller who thought he had spotted Elizabeth at a library. An officer allegedly checked out a homeless man wearing robes and his two female companions, one a young girl behind a veil—much like the garb worn by Smart and her alleged captors the day they were found in March 2003.

According to the Associated Press, Salt Lake Police Chief Rick Dinse had no intentions of reading the book or commenting on it. But, Elizabeth's father said she was being forced to relive her kidnapping ordeal by the publication of the book. He told the Associated Press that she read the book, and that both the words and the main cover photograph brought back memories of her abduction. He said she had already been through enough.

Tom Smart answered his brother's criticism by telling the Associated Press, "I understand it is a traumatic experience, and in reading the book, I still cry through the last third of it. I can understand Elizabeth wanting to put it behind her."

The cover of the book shows Elizabeth as she was when found, as a fourteen-year-old under a veil. Tom Smart told the Associated Press that his brother and his wife Lois received an advance copy of the book but refused to read it.

Elizabeth's father said his family is not endorsing the book because "we feel like Elizabeth has her own story she hasn't ever told anyone. We don't know that she ever will."

But, despite the rift over the book, the brothers went public to say it would not cause any long-lasting hurt within the family. "It's been hard, but we love and appreciate all the family did," Ed Smart told the Associated Press.

"I wrote this with every page in mind that someday Elizabeth would read it. I love my brother, Elizabeth, and Lois. The rest of my family has felt strongly that this was a story that needed to be told," Tom said.

In a March 27, 2003, article written by Marci Hamilton on findlaw.com, she questions the type of media coverage given to the kidnapping: "Elizabeth Smart's rescue from her abductor, Brian David Mitchell—a fundamentalist extremist who kidnapped her to make her one of his seven divine wives—has been the subject of intense press coverage. But that coverage has been curiously circumscribed."

Over and over again, analogies had been made to the Patty Hearst case. Like Smart, Hearst was a girl apparently brainwashed by her captors. But there are significant differences between the two cases. First, Smart was sexually assaulted by an adult, which should have led to stories about the psychological effects on children of repeated sexual abuse by adults in control of them.

Second, the brainwasher in Smart's case used religious brainwashing, which should have brought to mind the charges brought against the Reverend Moon's Unification Church and suicide cults such as that of Jim Jones. Religious brainwashing can be extraordinarily powerful and dangerous to those who are either too young or too disabled to withstand the religious pressure.

Brainwashing, particularly religious brainwashing, is a phenomenon about which Americans are largely in denial. The law is in denial too. Hamilton questions why the religious brainwashing analogy had not been explored in the media.

> One answer may be that it is very difficult for Americans to come to terms with the fact that religious individuals and organizations can willfully harm others. This kind of denial may explain why it took decades for the media to break the extent of the Catholic clergy abuse scandal. It may also explain why it is still the case that precious few are covering with the vigor it demands from the perspective of the public— and especially the children's—good. Another answer may be that there is a second level of denial here, because Americans have a fundamental belief in free will. To those with that belief, brainwashing is especially terrifying, because it involves the loss of the core of individual liberty.

According to Hamilton, children, as well as emotionally or mentally disabled adults, have a serious risk of being subject to manipulation, especially when it involves religion.

Smart was devout to begin with. Mitchell professed to practice a purer
version of her own religion. He claimed a divine revelation had shown
him [that] he should take her as his wife. He changed her name to one
he had chosen. And all the while, he espoused his own eccentric version of Mormon fundamentalism. The press has given us these few
facts in outline, leaving the previous religious brainwashing cases to
the side, and, further, it has done precious little to further explore the
dynamics of the sexual element of the sort of crime suffered by Smart.

Did the media adequately cover Elizabeth Smart's abduction?

Not according to David Mattingly at CNN.com. On August 14,
2002, he asked the question, "Missing kids: Has media coverage been
fair?"

In his story, he discusses Elizabeth's disappearance, referred to
as every parent's nightmare, being the story of the summer, with daily
continuing coverage by most national news outlets:

Yet weeks before 14-year-old Elizabeth's abduction became the nightmare of the Smart family, the parents of Alexis Patterson already had
faced their own nightmare. The 7-year-old Milwaukee girl vanished
one morning in May after leaving for school. The parents of Wesley
Dale Morgan also had faced their own nightmare. The 2-year-old boy
was last seen playing with puppies a year ago in his front yard in Clin-
ton, Louisiana. Both those cases of missing children received substan-
tially less national coverage than Elizabeth Smart's abduction.

Mattingly then quoted Alexis's stepfather LaRon Bourgeois as
saying,

"Everybody knows about Elizabeth Smart and that's not fair. Give ours
just as much airtime as you give her everywhere. I mean these kids are
helpless. What can they do? What can they do?" It has been suggested
that the amount of national media attention given to a case may depend
on the parent's ability to get the media's interest. "It has a lot to do with
how media savvy they are and how willing they are to put themselves
before the media," said Al Cross, president of the Society of Professional Journalists.

Mattingly goes on to explain,

But once in front of the media, a family's home life and economic status comes into play as well—factors that can make it more difficult for
a mass audience to relate to the story. If this is true, then it may have
been Elizabeth Smart's abduction in the night from a picture perfect

neighborhood and seemingly secure home that made her story so compelling to so many people. What also made it attractive to many experts is the story's simplicity. "The simpler the story can be told and the more appealing it is to basic emotions without complicating factors, the more appealing it probably is," said Cross.

In the case of a missing child, such complicating factors may possibly be the difference between a national headline and national obscurity.

Writing for the Center for Integration and Improvement of Journalism on www.ciij.org, Akilah Monifa said news organizations need to cover missing kids regardless of ethnicity or economics.

> Approximately every week I receive a flyer from the National Center for Missing & Exploited Children, a 501(c)(3) nonprofit organization. There are always two pictures of missing folks, usually children. Years ago, missing children's pictures used to be on milk cartons. Rarely are any of the missing people folks of color. Likewise, much media attention has recently been given to the disappearance of Elizabeth Smart, as well as the disappearance and killing of Samantha Runnion. That any person, much less a child, is missing, molested, and/or murdered is truly tragic. But it is interesting to note the media coverage of these events and the interplay of race.

Monifa also brings up the case of Alexis Patterson, who was kidnapped a month before Elizabeth and who, she writes, received virtually no coverage in the mainstream media.

> According to Charlie McCollum of the San Jose *Mercury News*, in the same time frame stories about Smart versus Patterson ran 1,000 to 100. Heck, even JonBenet Ramsey, some five-and-a-half years later, gets more press than a missing, kidnapped, or murdered child of color. So clearly, the mainstream news media depictions in terms of both coverage at all and airtime do not accurately reflect what is happening. If so, only white kids are missing, kidnapped and/or murdered, and only African-American men get beat up by the police (particularly if there is a video camera present to record the beating).

She goes on to ask, what does the mainstream media coverage of these children say about how children of color are valued in our society, and why don't children of color get similar coverage?

> Are we surprised when a child of color living in the inner city gets harmed in some way? But what is the shock value of a kid like Elizabeth Smart getting kidnapped from a gated community in Salt Lake City, Utah? Salt Lake is supposed to be safe, particularly gated communities. The inner city is supposed to be dangerous, so the fact

that children are harmed there isn't the breaking news. And certainly the Smarts have available a full barrage of legal counsel and communications folk, along with the access to the mainstream news media. So they can tell their story with ease and maximum print and broadcast coverage. As a general rule, both race and class exclude folks of color from accessing the same press machinery.

Monifa states that she believes the ultimate responsibility for media coverage, whether it be air time or print, is made by decision makers who, she claims, are mostly white.

> The few remaining media outlets can decide to examine their own race and class biases and look for stories beyond those easily presented to them by families of those privileged to have easy access to the press. They can go beyond Elizabeth Smart, Polly Klaas and Amber Schwartz and look for and give equal coverage to Alexis Patterson, Sherrice Iverson and countless other anonymous children of color who are missing or killed. The privileges afforded by media access cannot be changed, but the media's self-critique and inclusion around race and class can be. It is about balance and examination. Here's hoping that no child, regardless of color will need press.

Answers.com agrees, stating, "Some advocates have raised objections to the media tendency to focus so much attention on pretty Caucasian, blonde, blue-eyed girls like Smart, when so many other missing children do not receive the same level of media coverage. Media critics charged that a black, Asian, Latino, male or even ugly child would not have had any national media exposure after the first 24 hours."

Obviously the coverage of the Smart case and other cases leaves open questions.

## DISCUSSION QUESTIONS

1. What made the Elizabeth Ann Smart case so appealing to the media?
2. Should there be a way for other missing children to get some type of media coverage?
3. Should the media be accountable for their coverage of missing children?
4. How were the Smarts successful in manipulating the media?
5. Do money and status influence the media coverage of missing children?

# 14

# Scott Peterson, 2002

Why would a missing pregnant woman make national headlines? The answer to that may never be known, but the resulting almost daily coverage had a very tangible effect on public opinion. Consequently, when her husband went to trial, there was no way to effectively gauge to what degree that opinion influenced its outcome. The case is also important in that it clearly shows how interest groups can manipulate the media. While covering a major crime, the competition among media outlets becomes intense. Anything related to the crime, therefore, can become part of the story. Media-savvy groups have learned to take advantage of this and often push their causes by spinning their story to be part of the bigger crime story. The Scott Peterson case is a prime example of this.

Scott Peterson was guilty. At least, that was the obvious view of a news-starved media that had come upon a story that would keep the interest of the public. Perhaps it was a slow news week, or an editor just liked something about the story, but once one paper picked it up, it wasn't long before everyone got on the media bandwagon.

For one and a half years before the case ever came to trial, every detail of thirty-one-year-old Scott Peterson's life with his wife, Laci, and their unborn child was made public. Peterson was a fertilizer salesman from Modesto, a small town in California. His wife disappeared on Christmas Eve, 2002. He reported his wife missing the next afternoon.

Police said he killed her, weighted her body down with cement anchors, and dumped her in San Francisco Bay sometime around Christmas Eve. Peterson's attorney said she was abducted near her home, killed, and dumped in the bay to frame Peterson. They accused the police of a shoddy investigation, ignoring leads that would clear their client. They said the police were only out to prove him guilty.

The bodies of Laci and her unborn son were found in April 2003. Relatives and friends all gave their own versions of what happened, and almost every word was snatched up by the media and made public. A media circus ensued: who could get the best interview, who had the best leads, who could get exclusives.

The fetus, found with Laci's body, was quickly given a name, Connor, making him the second victim. The scenes of where the bodies were discovered were played over and over again. The body bag being removed and placed in a morgue van became the background for almost every television story on Peterson.

There were public disputes over autopsy results and if or how the bodies were mutilated. The murder was tried in the realm of public opinion. The stage was set to ensure public interest.

> It's hard to imagine a more hellish crime than a man murdering his young wife and their unborn son. But that's what California law-enforcement authorities believe Scott Peterson did. On Christmas Eve, his wife, Laci, a mother-to-be with an infectious smile, disappeared from their home in Modesto. Last Monday, California police announced that the decomposed bodies of a petite woman and full-term male fetus had washed up on a shore line some 90 miles northwest. Four days later, officials identified the victims as Laci and her child and arrested Scott for their murder. "The waiting this week has been horrific," said Kim Petersen, a spokeswoman for the dead woman's family. "I don't know if relief is the right word. They have answers." No doubt they also have painful questions. What happened? What darkness lurked beneath the happy surface of Laci and Scott's marriage? (Bower, 2003)

It would have been difficult to find anybody who had not read something about the case or did not have some kind of opinion about it. The media frenzy showed no signs of stopping. There was always a new angle. Adding to the hype, Peterson's alleged mistress, Amber Frey, held press conferences and hired a high-powered attorney. The prosecution suddenly decided not to call her at pretrial, but the defense team said they would call her as a witness.

The trial only brought on more media coverage. "For a year and a half, the deaths of Laci Peterson and her fetus have been the most talked-about crimes in America, with every detail, true or supposed, picked apart on television, in newspapers and over bowls of popcorn on living room couches" (Murphy, 2004).

Finally, in June 2004, the case officially moved from the public domain into the courtroom. It was court mandated that the press conferences be left behind. Meanwhile, a new stage was opened for the media. Hundreds of reporters covered the trial, but the atmosphere differed from the O.J. Simpson trial.

"Not only has Judge Alfred Delucchi placed a strict gag order on all participants, but the trial is taking place in Redwood City, Calif.— a town of Silicon Valley commuters with little interest in a murder case from almost 100 miles away. One edition of the local paper last week gave the Peterson trial less play than a story about a stray cat that had tied up traffic on Route 101" (Taylor, 2004).

But the media already knew the case's impact. "The trial had originally been set to take place in Modesto, but was moved here after a judge there determined Mr. Peterson could not have a fair trial. Even here in San Mateo County, about 15 miles south of San Francisco, it took three months to whittle through the pool of potential jurors to find 12 who had not made up their minds about Mr. Peterson's guilt or innocence" (Murphy, 2004).

It did not take long for a juror to be dismissed who had been joking with Laci's brother. Peterson's attorney, Mark Geragos, then demanded a new trial, saying the media coverage had tainted his case. His request was denied. However, in the court of public opinion, Peterson was clearly already tried and convicted. The public saw him as an unfaithful husband who killed his wife and unborn son. They also needed to know every gruesome detail.

A *New York Times* article best described the scene at the courthouse as two trials being held, one inside the courtroom and the other outside, where "a spin zone relentlessly churns before television cameras, which are barred from the courtroom itself. This one has drama and humor and pathos, played out breathlessly almost every day on Court TV and Fox News, on *Today* and *Larry King Live*. The outcome of this trial was decided long ago, though the courtroom proceeding is not half finished" (Waxman, 2004).

When the judge barred cameras, ambitious reporters turned to e-mail messages through wireless modems and BlackBerry wireless devices. Intermediaries sent messages to circumvent the judge's orders not to discuss the case.

But the trial is a necessary part of American life—one of a series of private tragedies that take on public proportions that feed the need for national spectacle—then the media have found a way to make it reliable entertainment. Despite all efforts by the judge to maintain decorum— even gum chewing was forbidden in the courtroom—the media maw is insatiable, and hardly picky about how to feed the beast. . . . Desperate, the television news pack has turned to self-proclaimed experts to tell *the* story of the day, every day. That spin, many producers said, is usually determined by the first break in the trial, at 10:30 A.M., almost no matter what happens later. (Waxman)

Peterson was convicted on November 12, 2004.

Outside, a crowd of several hundred people let out a roar when news of the verdict hit the street. Reporters and crews from several hundred news organizations were in and around the courthouse. Local newspapers printed special editions; the *Redwood City Daily News* had papers ready at the courthouse with the headlines "Guilty" and "Crowds Cheer Verdict." Some television stations had offered to send notice of the verdict by instant message to mobile phones. (Marshall, 2004)

Even the *New York Times* had it as their lead story in the National Report. The media compared this trial to O.J.'s, saying the public felt as if, this time, justice had been served.

Marty Kaplan, an associate dean at the University of Southern California, said, "We do have the ability in real time to present lurid trials as though they were already movies of the week. The only thing we're lacking as we tell it is knowing what the ending is" (Marshall, 2004).

In December, the sentencing phase of his trial began. Peterson's mother tearfully begged for her son's life, and his father tried to convince the jurors his son was not a monster. A Web site was set up on vote-america.org so people could vote if they thought Scott should get the death sentence. On December 13, 2004, the jury decided he should be put to death. On March 16, 2005, Judge Alfred A. Delucchi officially sentenced Scott Peterson to death.

When there are high-profile trials, like Peterson's, even the lawyers are affected. Attorney Leslie Abramson, who lost the Menendez brothers' murder trial, said that Mark Geragos, Peterson's attorney, would come back after his loss in the Peterson trial. "Once your name's out there, it's out there," Abramson said. But she warned of the pitfalls of pursuing celebrity cases. "Mark doesn't care about money, but he did care about fame," she said. "Sometimes when you pursue that beast, it eats you" (Deutsch, 2004).

Unbelievably, in November 2003, only seven months after Laci's body was found, the first of many books was published on the crime. *Laci, Inside the Laci Peterson Murder* by Michael Fleeman took media coverage and summarized it for the general public.

Other authors quickly got on the publishing bandwagon. In July 2004, *The Murder of Laci Peterson: The Inside Story of What Really*

*Happened* was written by Clifford L. Lindecker. Television shows depicted the crime. A DVD entitled *Perfect Husband—The Laci Peterson Story* was released in December 2004. And, if you really wanted the whole story, *Laci Peterson: The Whole Story*, by Brad Knight, was also released in December 2004.

Not to be outdone, Amber Frey was quick to get a book out on her own, before other members of the family could follow suit. Her book, published in January 2005, was preceded by numerous media interviews and celebrity treatment. In the book, she maintained she had a strong religious belief, and that she was convinced that she had been chosen to be Laci's voice. Amber writes:

> I've never met Laci Peterson, and all I'd ever seen of her was a grainy photograph on the Internet. But I wanted to help her. I wanted to believe that she and her child were alive and that I could keep them alive and bring them home safely. It was the oddest feeling: I thought Laci Peterson needed me; I thought she was counting on me to bring her and her baby home.

Her chapter headings tell the book's story:

"Can I trust you with my heart?"

"'Please God, tell me it's not the same Scott Peterson."

"We have been praying for someone like you to come forward."

"Oh my God! Laci's baby is due on my birthday!"

"Isn't that a little twisted, Scott?"

"I know I'm innocent, they know I'm innocent, everyone close to this knows I'm innocent."

"Goodbye for now."

"The day you went to the police you became Laci's voice."

"I can do everything through Him who gives me strength."

Was Amber another innocent victim of Scott Peterson? And if she was, there is a resulting moral question of financial gain and celebrity status. Was she a victim, or motivated by greed?

In her book, she says she still thinks about Scott and wonders if he still thinks about her. In an attempt to sell her book on Amazon.com, the product description ends with, "Witness the chilling story of how a young woman became ensnared in Scott Peterson's web of lies, and then risked everything to seek justice for Laci Peterson and her unborn child, Connor."

During almost every media interview, Amber cried. The tears looked real, but the repeated use of them could cause questions as to the emotions behind them.

Despite her successful publicity tour, her appearance on almost every network across the country, and successful book sales, not everyone was pleased with the book. According to John Cote, a staff writer on modbee.com, Laci's parents were upset by the book's cover, which depicted a large glamorous color photo of Amber and two smaller black and white photos of Laci over one shoulder and Scott over the other. According to his January 4, 2005 story, the attorney for Laci's family, Adam Stewart, said the family found the cover "extremely hurtful and offensive to Laci's mother and her family." He added, "Displaying a picture of Laci on the cover of Amber Frey's book portrays a lack of respect and insensitivity towards Laci and Laci's family and friends."

What was also not highlighted by the media as they embraced Amber was that she had testified that Peterson never tried to stop her from going to the police about their affair, and that he had never told her that he loved her.

Only two months later, Scott's sister, who had been put up for adoption when she was a baby, decided to write her own book, entitled *Blood Brother: 33 Reasons My Brother Scott Peterson Is Guilty*. The same month, Catherine Crier, a former judge and television legal analyst, wrote *A Deadly Game: The Untold Story of the Scott Peterson Investigation*.

All three women would become wealthy as a result of Laci's murder, as all three books made it to the *New York Times* best-seller list.

With all this coverage, the image of a guilty Scott Peterson is forever embedded in the mind of the American public. It would be difficult to tell if he had been tried on facts or prejudged opinion, but what is certain is that his actions made a lot of people very wealthy and very famous.

But his case and the resulting publicity had further implications. It could affect millions of women in this country. Four months after Scott was arrested and charged with killing his wife and their unborn son, President George Bush signed the Unborn Victims of Violence Act, which made it a federal offense to harm a fetus. According to a story in *Newsday*, conservatives acknowledged that the Peterson case provided the momentum to overcome the opposition. "Many feel that this law would be laying the groundwork for a significant reduction in the amount of abortions performed" (Sussman, 2005).

The media, in its frenzy to cover every aspect of the Scott Peterson case, may have aided the anti-abortion groups in the country. When Scott was charged with the murder of his unborn son, abortion advocates were in a difficult situation. How could they make an issue of this ruling? To do so would only incite the media even more. And so, they made a careful decision not to say anything, despite the fact that they strongly disagreed. While they remained quiet, abortion foes took the opportunity to push though the Unborn Victims of Violence Act. In choosing this case to relentlessly focus on, the media might have become a useful tool in the movement to ban abortions in the United States.

"Spectators outside a California courthouse cheered when Scott Peterson was convicted in November of killing his wife and unborn son, but women's groups are less than gleeful over fallout from the case, saying conservatives are using it to promote anti-abortion laws as they shun legislation to stem violence against women" (Susman, 2005). The story goes on to say that while conservatives had tried for five years to pass the Unborn Victims act, the Peterson case provided the momentum to overcome the opposition.

A lot of money was made, people became famous, and a young mother and her unborn child were murdered. Once again, in the end, the victims appear to disappear from the limelight, and those who benefit, whether the media or the participants, quickly take over.

A ray of hope did come through. Paul Campos, a law professor at the University of Colorado, published a column on a local Web site:

> Consider this very partial list of names, . . . Terri, Ashley, Laci, Amber, Elizabeth, Chandra, . . . JonBenet and now Jennifer, the runaway bride. . . . Some of these stories were genuine tragedies and some were merely melodramas, but all have two things in common. First, none of them deserved one-tenth of the coverage they received, if newsworthiness is measured by either the public importance or the uniqueness of the news involved. Second, and not coincidentally, the average American knows far more about each of these stories—and indeed can identify most of them from nothing more than the first name . . .—than he or she does about, say, the battle over Social Security.

Campos attempts to put into perspective why the media gets hold of one story and seemingly never lets go: "Of course our news industry has an all-purpose excuse for this state of affairs. 'We don't decide what people want to hear about,' the priests of the media declare. 'We are but humble servants of The Market, which speaks through its oracle: Ratings.'"

In the end, the news media covers crime based on ratings. As more people watch, the particular crime being covered subtly changes as the public's opinion becomes stronger, leading to the question that the media would be reluctant to answer—is crime news, or merely entertainment?

There are times that the media does question itself:

> What is the fascination with Laci Peterson, JonBenet Ramsey and now Jennifer Wilbanks? Are suspected crimes against young women the only news worth covering? Isn't news that might affect our lives, like taxes or national security, a better use of time and effort? Yet, when cable outlets chose to focus on the latest bikini-clad teacher having an affair with a 14-year-old student, such vital issues get lost in the shuffle. (Gainsvilletimes.com, 2005)

So, who is really to blame: the media or the public?

## DISCUSSION QUESTIONS

1. What was the fascination to the media of the Scott Peterson story?
2. Did Scott Peterson get a fair trial?
3. If the case had escaped media coverage, how would it have been different?
4. Did Amber Frey take advantage of her time in the media spotlight, or was she a victim as well?
5. What about Peterson sister? What do you think her motives were for writing her book?
6. Do you think the anti-abortion advocates took unfair advantage of this tragedy to further their own cause? And if so, did the media play into their agenda?

# CHAPTER

# 15

# Michael Jackson, 2004

The trial of Michael Jackson holds a major place in the study of media coverage of celebrity trials. When the decision was made to do a daily reenactment of the trial, media coverage was brought to a new level. On its own, this was a way to influence the public and potentially the jury, but add to that the Jackson fans, as well as those who knew enough about him to strongly dislike him, and the ground was set for a trial that was clearly played in the realm of public opinion. This was a trial that was not simply about an alleged child molester; it was about a celebrity, and in today's society, with extensive, unrestricted media coverage, can a celebrity get a fair trial?

The trial of Michael Jackson might long be remembered, not so much for what happened, but for the fact that the coverage was the first to almost rival that of the O.J. Simpson case. The major difference was that television cameras were not allowed in the courtroom, but that certainly did not stop the press. The E! cable channel announced its plans to do daily reenactments, with actors playing Jackson, the lawyers, and the witnesses. If you could not get the so-called news at the moment it happened, then why not just reenact it? All of this was a sure sign that the gap between news and entertainment is rapidly becoming smaller.

The trial was as bizarre as Jackson himself. Almost equally bizarre was the *New York Times* deeming it so newsworthy, they gave it almost daily coverage. Jackson was accused of molesting a thirteen-year-old boy at his Neverland ranch. He was also charged with giving the boy alcohol and conspiring to hold the boy's family captive to rebut a commentary in which Jackson said he shared a bed with children.

Many things about the case made it unique. For example, according to *Time* magazine, by January 2004, it had already cost the county $75,000 for expenses related to the trial. A $250 daily rate was charged to the media for parking spaces outside the courtroom to defray these costs.

On November 20, 2003, it was first announced that Jackson faced arrest. The *New York Times* took on this story with a vengeance and followed through with almost daily coverage. On November 20, there was an article on the front page, which continued onto a full-page spread in the National Report. Another article was written for the Fine Arts section. In addition to details of the arrest warrant, they printed a story on Jackson's financial status, CBS's dropping of his television special, and an analysis of the trial.

> One of the oddest things about Michael Jackson is that this 45-year-old former Motown child prodigy has remained a superstar despite all the Peter Pan fantasies, Potemkin marriages, cosmetic surgery, spending sprees and now criminal charges of child molestation. He is both a popular entertainer and a tabloid freak show. In that sense he is the perfect icon for the shame-free age: a television twofer. . . . Television forgives almost any misstep, mainly because any misstep can be transformed into entertainment. (Stanley, 2003 p. E1)

From the beginning, it was reported that Jackson fought back in his own way. "The bad blood between Michael Jackson and the prosecutor who filed child molestation charges against him goes back more than a decade. It even spawned a song in which the pop star calls Santa Barbara County District Attorney Tom Sneddon a 'cold man'" (*Newsday*, 2003).

In 1993, a civil allegation had been brought against Jackson by Sneddon in which he was accused of molesting a twelve-year-old boy. That case was closed when Jackson reportedly made a $20 million settlement.

On November 21, 2003, after Jackson was booked on the molestation charges, the *New York Times* again took over half a page and made it the lead story. "To judge from the media coverage—the instant prime-time specials; the nonstop frenzy on CNN and in the newspapers; the rapid, rabid airing of the most lurid speculation—you would think Michael Jackson's arrest on charges of molesting a twelve-year-old boy was the surprise ending of a story rather than the next and perhaps last act in a tale that threatens to carry with it a tragic inevitability" (Corliss, 2003).

Two days later, it made a lead story for the National Report and over half a page again in the *New York Times*, only this time the focus was on Jackson's attorneys. Mark Geragos, who had unsuccessfully defended Scott Peterson, was now part of Jackson's defense team. Dealing with both cases had made him an instant celebrity. "There were so many calls to his pager—over 700 over one 24-hour period this week, including about 620 from reporters—that the pager became disabled, he said" (Murphy, p. 20).

Even before Jackson was formally booked, there was speculation in the press. The *New York Times* reported that child welfare officials in Los Angeles County did not believe that Jackson was guilty. They credited a leaked memorandum, which they reported had first appeared on The Smoking Gun Web site (LeDuff, 2003).

Jackson was formally booked on December 18, 2004, and the next day, the story again took the lead in the National Report in the *New York Times*. More than 100 reporters covered D.A. Sneddon's press conference, in which he revealed that Jackson was being charged with seven counts of child molesting and two counts of giving a minor an intoxicating agent. Statements were released by Jackson's attorneys and his family.

What would a high-profile case be without the now routine media leaks? "Twice in the past month, sensitive grand jury material from high-profile investigations has found its way into the hands of the news media, setting off a collision between the rights of the accused and the First Amendment. In the past week, extensive excerpts from grand jury material in the Michael Jackson child molestation case were posted on thesmokinggun.com Web site and broadcast on ABC news" (Broder, 2004).

Leaking information from a grand jury could potentially prejudice a jury, but the media argued that this information should be public. When someone's future or even life is on the line, does the media have a right to argue the merits of a free press versus an unbiased jury?

Meanwhile, the judge continued to try to keep a tight lid on the case. Ted Boutrous, who represented a group of media organizations, tried to get the judge to be more lenient in releasing documents.

> "The time has come . . . to let the sun shine in so the public, and the press as its surrogates, can know what the case is about," Boutrous said. . . . During the sparring, the judge admitted to feeling aggravated by the situation caused by Jackson's notoriety. "You need not mislead the public and press that I'm doing something against the law. The difficulty of seeing that an individual in this country gets a fair trial is exasperating when the individual is known around the world," Melville told the attorneys, adding that he was "being very careful in following the law." (Grossberg, 2004)

Is it possible, in this country, for a celebrity to get a fair trial? For that matter, is it possible for any person whom the media picks to "celebritize," for whatever reason, to get a fair trial?

These were serious charges for Jackson. He faced one count of conspiracy to commit child abduction and attempted lewd acts upon a child, four counts of committing lewd acts upon a child, and four counts of administering intoxicating agents to assist in commission of a felony. The maximum jail time was twenty or more years. By the end of January, the Associated Press was reporting that Jackson was condemning recent media leaks and calling them disgusting and false. He said all he wanted was a fair trial (Associated Press, January 30, 2004). On Sunday, January 30, Jackson made a preemptive move and released a videotape that was approved by the judge. He responded to the grand jury leaks and denied all the accusations against him. The media was anxiously awaiting the beginning of the trial: a trial that focused on the defendant, not the victim.

In April 2004, Jackson publicly announced he was replacing his high-profile legal team. That brought on more media speculation. The *New York Times* in one of their lead stories in the National Report reported, "Mr. Jackson, 45, has long been surrounded by his family members, including his parents and his brothers, with whom he performed as a child as a member of the Jackson 5 before starting his successful solo career. He has also more recently been advised by leaders of the Nation of Islam and others who have advocated a more aggressive response to the current allegations" (Broder, 2004, p. A14).

The trial had turned into a bizarre play, with an increasing audience of media representatives who fought for the best seats and the best angles. "But it does promise to be a show—a media onslaught befitting a man who has been a global superstar since his childhood, reenactments of daily testimony on cable television and a pitched battle inside the courtroom as Jackson tries to avoid 20 or more years in prison" (Riley, 2005, p. A14).

But what about the trial, the true essence of our legal system? Was this a show, or was it a display of events to be supersized by the media?

Remember when being charged with child molestation was a bad thing? In a spectacle that even hardened TV-news commentators described as a freak show, pop star Michael Jackson appeared in a Santa Maria, California, court to plead not guilty to seven counts of lewd acts with a child and two counts of giving intoxicants to a child. Outside, hundreds of fans—some of whom arrived on buses chartered by Jackson's camp—screamed their support while Jackson's bodyguards handed out invitations to the star's Neverland Ranch for postarraignment festivities. Later, Jackson climbed onto the roof of his black SUV, clapped his hands and danced a few steps. He must be saving the moonwalk for the preliminary hearing. (Song, 2005)

On January 30, 2005, *Newsday* did a two-page spread on Jackson. It was only the beginning of almost daily media coverage of his trial. On January 31, the jury selection was scheduled to begin.

> Nearly 1,000 reporters, photographers, television technicians, and courtroom artists have applied for credentials to cover the trial which will be reenacted nightly by a combined British-American television group that includes E! Entertainment. Months of pretrial maneuverings have already produced thousands of pages of legal pleadings and teased a global audience awaiting the lurid details of Mr. Jackson's extravagant and eccentric life at his 2,700-acre private Xanadu in the hills between Santa Maria and Santa Barbara. The case itself offers all the elements of pop culture roundelay, including a music superstar who likens himself to Peter Pan; a grandfatherly prosecutor who has pursued him for 12 years; a silver-maned chief defense lawyer who is a colorful defender of the famous and the downtrodden alike; and a scandal-saturated media horde, many of them fresh from the Scott Peterson murder case. And throngs of Jackson groupies are promising daily courthouse rallies. (Broder, January 31, 2005, p. A17)

Without Scott Peterson to cover, the media needed a new cause. They obviously had found one.

The jury selection began as scheduled on February 1, 2005. But there was an overriding question that still remained—could Jackson get a fair trial? The first obstacle would be to pick the jury. "The court will have a challenge assembling a jury of Mr. Jackson's peers.[1] It is unlikely that the county has 12 citizens who live in an amusement park—he calls his ranch Neverland—who have made and spent hundreds of millions of dollars and whose appearances have changed radically over the past 20 years" (Broder & LeDuff, p. A12).

In addition, the city of Santa Maria spent $18,000 to build a chain link fence around the courtroom to contain the reporters and spectators, and expected police overtime to cost $40,000 a month (*Time* Magazine Notebook, 2005).

"More than 1,000 journalists applied for press credentials, but only seven seats in the courtroom [were] reserved for reporters" (Ressner, 2005). The town knew it was going to change.

---

[1] Of course, a jury of your peers means nothing but a cross section of members of any community.

But the trial has thrown things off kilter. The media trucks and Jackson's convoy of black sport utility vehicles clog roads and snap up parking spaces. Residents are startled by the men wearing makeup—television reporters—in their steakhouses and parking lots. . . . Some Santa Marians say they're sick of the hoopla of the trial. But others are clearly enthralled by the spectacle of dozens of media tents and a possibility of Jackson sighting. (Searcey, March 7, 2005, p. A16)

For the local residents, the press coverage became their own show. "The news media, as is now the norm in celebrity trials, was the main spectacle on Monday morning, numbering about 500 print and broadcast reporters. One foreign television crew was doing its broadcast of the Iraqi elections from the courthouse parking lot. A reporter said, 'Everything in this case is special; everything is different'" (Broder & LeDuff, p. A12). The *New York Times* even did an article on Jackson's clothing.

Jury selection, which was expected to last several weeks, took only five days. The trial began on Monday, February 28, 2005. Judge Rodney Melville quickly set the tone. He ordered Jackson to be on time and set strict guidelines for his courtroom.

It was already clear that Mr. Jackson's trial will not be a replay of the 1995 televised trial of O.J. Simpson, which Judge Lance Ito at times seemed powerless to control. Judge Melville is not allowing cameras in his courtroom and has barred all lawyers and witnesses from public discussion of the case. . . . The judge gave a small insight into his feelings about the Jackson case as jury selection began three weeks ago. Addressing the pool of potential jurors, he confessed to a case of the jitters at presiding over such a closely watched case, saying that not only Mr. Jackson, but the entire American legal system was on trial. (Broder, February 25, 2005, p. A14)

In March, almost every daily newspaper in the country covered the daily proceedings as the prosecution, led by District Attorney Thomas Sneddon, Jr., paraded witnesses before the jury, including people who had worked for Jackson, relatives of the young boy, Jackson's ex-wife, and the accuser himself. Comedian Jay Leno, who had been subpoenaed, requested the judge to lift or clarify a gag order that appeared to keep him from using the Jackson trial in his comedy routine. In March, the judge ruled that he could crack all the jokes he wanted, and in his own comeback, the judge said, "I'd like him to tell good jokes . . . but I guess I can't control that" (Associated Press, March 11, 2005).

The media headlines continued to summarize the day's events. They revealed who would be the next to testify. They even revealed when the trial seemed to get "boring" when images from Jackson's pornography collection were showed to the jurors. Every move by Jackson was being covered by the press. On March 11, when Jackson was late, the *New York Times* had a picture of him arriving at court in the center of the front page. This was surrounded by headlines that read, "Pentagon Seeks to Shift Inmates from Cuba Base," "U.S. and Allies Agree on Steps in Iran Dispute," and "How to Unite Congress, Spend Billions on Roads." In the middle of it all is Jackson in his pajamas. Was that really so important?

> Maybe it really was a lightning attack of back spasms that kept Michael Jackson out of court last week. (It's plausible.) Or maybe he just thought the event thus far had been short on melodrama. (It hadn't.) But on Thursday, when he finally appeared in Santa Barbara County Superior Court after the judge in the child-molestation case threatened to revoke his $3 million bail, the deposed King of Pop displayed his usual showmanship, even if not his usual sartorial flair. Wearing a dark jacket over blue pajama bottoms, and supported by bodyguards, the 46-year-old moonwalker did a slow, frail moon swoon past the gaggle of reporters. . . . Jackson has treated the trial as an occasion for his performance art—arriving fashionably late, as if to his own concert, doling out gallery seats to his family and the lingering faithful, some of whom are sleeping over at the Gloved One's Neverland estate, where the crimes are alleged to have occurred. (Corliss, 2005, p. 56)

On Monday, March 28, the judge ruled that the jury could hear allegations that the one-time star had molested other boys, including actor Macaulay Culkin. They also revealed that two other young men had reached multimillion-dollar settlements with Jackson.

On May 4, 2005, the prosecution completed their case. The prosecution had called more than 80 witnesses over almost nine weeks, some appearing to help the defense more. The Jackson team asked for the charges to be dismissed. The judge denied their motion.

The media would continue to incessantly cover the story. With this kind of media coverage, there are always people who will make money, in one way or another. This case was no different.

> A local lawyer is charging TV cameramen thousands of dollars for a prime spot on his roof where they can train their lenses on Michael Jackson walking in and out of court. Legal experts have come from as far away as New York and Seattle to pontificate for reporters—and to benefit from free advertising for their firms. Actor Gary Coleman is also trying to cash in, showing up to crack Jackson jokes on the All Comedy Radio Network. Even in the throes of a molestation trial, everybody it

seems, wants something from Michael Jackson. . . . At the office of attorney Michael B. Clayton, situated across the street from the courthouse, everything is for sale; his parking lot, phone lines and roof space, which goes for $2,700, to cameramen angling for a better view of Jackson. Clayton, a Jackson supporter who estimates he's earned $250,000 from the media since the charges were brought last year, said anyone who criticizes him for making money off the case is just jealous. "It's not an outrage," he said. "It's business smarts." (Searcey, April 4, 2005, p. A8)

With the trial only half over, an online casino betting site started taking bets on the outcome of the Jackson trial. They offered odds on a variety of different possible outcomes.

There were those who began to question the coverage. "Fans, not just children, have to ask one more question: Why must our stars fall so spectacularly and fail us so egregiously? The suspicion here is, because we want them to. Indeed, it may be the prime instructive function of celebrities to show us, in their early radiance, what we could dream of being—and in the murk of their decline, what we fear, or know, we could become" (Corliss, December 1, 2003). The media feeds into what the public wants; the public wants them to fail.

"The Michael Jackson case, and the kidnapped bride who really ran away. Both of those stores are so perfect for cable news that the more conspiratorial-minded could be forgiven for suspecting that they are actually reality TV shows disguised as news events" (Campos, 2005).

There were things that made this trial unique.

The days when America gathered around the TV set to watch celebrities like O.J. Simpson on trial now seem as distant as *Father Knows Best*. The Michael Jackson case was the latest in a long string of recent high-profile cases—Martha Stewart, Scott Peterson, Kobe Bryant, Robert Blake, Bernie Ebbers and more—in which cameras have been banned or severely restricted. So desperate is TV for at least a semblance of in-court coverage that the E! cable channel did air daily re-enactments, with actors playing Jackson, the lawyers and the witnesses. (Zoglin, 2005, p. 15)

Playing to the jury, the media, and the public, Jackson was also alleged to build up the image of being a victim.

Michael Jackson has played the victim in his songs for years. In "Billie Jean," he portrays the target of a false paternity claim. In "Man in the Mirror," he says he's "been a victim of a selfish king of love." And throughout the album "HIStory," he's threatened by ominous characters such as "D.S.,"—a character based on the prosecutor now accusing him of child molestation. . . . Jackson will again present himself as a victim— but this time his attorneys say it's no performance. They say Jackson is the target of overzealous prosecutors, an untrustworthy inner circle and a family of drifters making false allegations. (Molloy, 2005)

But whether he was a victim or not, whether he received a fair trial or not, whether the media spectacle helped or hurt him, Jackson will no doubt suffer consequences as a result of this very public trial. A poll conducted by billboard.com revealed that Jackson's career as superstar would not survive his trial. Of 6,851 respondents, 45 percent said that no matter what the outcome, Jackson's image has been irreparably tarnished by the allegations (Cohen, 2005). And, so, perhaps, has the media's credibility.

And in an age of terrorism, it makes sense for journalists to balance the onslaught of depressing news with more sensational fare. But from Kobe to Jacko to Martha to Terri to Jennifer, balance is often obliterated as the networks smother their latest obsession, apparently fearful that changing subjects will cause viewers to click away. It's talk-radio version of news, a few facts surrounded by commentary, speculation, argument, angst, and a platform for anyone with a tangential connection to the controversy. (Kurtz, 2005, p. BO1)

Are the days of news coverage as we once knew it over? Has an exciting, "sexy" story now taken precedence over what might have been a more newsworthy event? And, more importantly, in the long run, who is affected? Certainly the person, or persons, who are the focus of this attention. But, perhaps even more important, so is the public. For as the media continually fights for the "public's right to know," the public is, in reality, knowing less and less.

Michael Jackson was acquitted on all counts. Though some of the jurors believe that he is guilty of molesting children, the evidence as presented was not enough for a conviction. While the jury was out, I (RM) had the opportunity to listen to the broadcasts on the BBC (in the United Kingdom). The reporters were appalled at the way this case was being handled and the publicity it had been receiving. They could not understand why, as the jury was out, there was a discussion in the press of "what ifs": What if Jackson were convicted; what would happen to his children; what plans were being made. But in the end it made no difference because Jackson was freed. What the future holds for Michael Jackson is anyone's guess, but we believe that there will be follow-up stories and many individuals will be more than glad to read on.

## DISCUSSION QUESTIONS

1. What effect did the daily re-enactment have on the outcome of the trial?

2. Can the media produce a "true" re-enactment, or is it merely their interpretation of the facts?

3. What role did the controversy surrounding Michael Jackson in the years prior to the trial have on the outcome?

4. Did the media have a predetermined image of the superstar?

5. Did the media's image affect the public's perception?

6. Do you think paper such as the *New York Times* should have played up the story as much as it did?

# 16

# Female Offenders Depicted by the Media

### *Krista Gehring*

When I was young, I loved to watch *Charlie's Angels*. My favorite episode was "Angels in Chains," in which Sabrina, Kelly, and Jill infiltrated a women's prison to bust up a prostitution ring. They got away from the evil sheriff and ran across perilous terrain while handcuffed together. At one point, Sabrina and Kelly were pulling in opposite directions, and Jill, stuck in the middle, screamed, "Hey, I'm not a yo-yo." They run off in their tight bellbottoms and unbuttoned denim shirts, steal a potato truck, and foil the bad police officers by throwing potatoes off that rickety truck, forcing the police cars off the road. Score another for the jiggly trio! Now all we have to look forward to are drinks back at the Townsend Agency and congratulations given to the women via speakerphone. What a way to undermine serious police work.

Our culture is greatly influenced by television; almost all of the information we receive flickers on the screen of the "magic box" in our living room. This is a problem: We are a captive audience of the major networks and only view information that they choose to give us at their discretion. The cliché phrase, "If it bleeds, it leads" is unfortunately the case with American media; the search for heinous, outrageous, and even "sexy" crimes (as mentioned throughout this work) is sure to boost ratings.

The American public must question the information that bombards us every day. People need to realize that they must look at mass media more critically. This is especially true when examining fictional portrayals of women in the criminal justice system or the sensationalization of crimes committed by female offenders.

Fictional portrayals of women in the criminal justice system confuse how the system and its players really work. One does not have to surf far before landing on a channel broadcasting one of the four *Law & Order*s or one of the three *CSI*s to see attractive female detectives and lawyers. In these programs, impossibly good-looking members of the criminal justice system solve crimes and prosecute criminals with such skill and drama that there is no question in the public's mind that this must all be true. The criminal justice system must look like this— it must really work the way it is portrayed on television. The women in these shows are smart, attractive, and impeccably dressed. They are sexy and alluring, regardless of their position in the criminal justice system. Attractive detectives, lawyers, and even victims keep us from changing the channel. The sex appeal of these characters keeps people watching, but this is far from reality. One wonders whether, in thirty years or so, we have really come that far from *Charlie's Angels*.

What could be more horrible than a woman killing her own children? A wife killing her husband? A prostitute killing her johns? A female nurse killing patients? The telling aspect of the criminalization of these women is that we know who they are. The names Susan Smith, Darlie Routier, and Andrea Yates are recognizable to most— these are mothers who did the unthinkable by killing their children. And what of Betty Broderick, Lorena Bobbitt, Aileen Wuornos, Jean Harris, and Mary Kay Letourneau? The data demonstrate, according to Gehring, that men commit these crimes at a greater rate, yet media sensationalizes the crimes these women commit because they are reinforcing a woman's place in society. Also, men commit crimes at a much greater rate; stories of them killing their wives and children, beating their wives, molesting children, and frequenting and possibly killing prostitutes are just too common to appeal to television audiences. Women have the needed sex appeal.

It is clear that the general public is getting incorrect information about women and the criminal justice system. People take what they see on television as truth, and these portrayals of fictional and actual women in the criminal justice system distort public perception of the actual reality. If we were to examine famous female criminals and why their cases have received so much media attention, we would find that these crimes are not intrinsically heinous; however, these women have been criminalized because their crimes have gone against our society's gender roles.

# 17

# A Star Is Formed

## Media Construction of the Female Criminal

### Krista Gehring

Based on recent television programming, Americans seem to be addicted to crime and television. They scour the television guides for the next *American Justice, Investigative Reports,* and *Forensic Files,* or one of the four *Law & Order* programs. Broadcasting networks have discovered that crime does pay. There is a particular series on Court TV called *Mugshots* that advertises itself as "an irresistible blend of crime and biography that offers in-depth profiles of the country's most notorious criminals." There have been "Mugshots" about Jeffrey Dahmer, Ted Bundy, and Charles Ng and Leonard Lake, so the viewer who settles in for the evening can learn about another infamous criminal and his or her grisly crimes.

But on this particular night the viewer was to be disappointed. Tonight's episode: Tonya Harding. Tonya Harding? The confused viewer grabbed the TV guide to read the program description: "This is the story of what happens when an ice maiden melts down and competition spins out of control. From iron bars to gold medals, from cold hearts to hired hands, this show takes you to the very heart of an all-American tragedy." *So dramatic.* There have been many American tragedies, but one must wonder if the Tonya Harding story can truly be called this. This viewer scratched her head and realized she could not remember the names of Tonya's bar-wielding male accomplices. Tonya Harding is the name Americans know, along with the names of other female offenders who have been made famous by the media.

One must take notice of all the women who have gotten so much media attention for their crimes, though they did not commit offenses that were as atrocious as those of their male counterparts. The crimes they committed were overcriminalized because they were women; a majority of crimes committed are not gender spe-cific, but the public is not aware, or is just not interested, if a man commits the same crime. Women who commit crimes are going against society's views of how women should behave. In American society, the culturally valued role for women has been that of wife and mother. Any departure from these gendered roles is believed to result in a disruption of social order. Women who deviate from traditional norms become outcasts and must be punished to set an example so other women are not tempted to do the same. The women discussed in this chapter have deviated from their gender roles; they are infamous because their crimes have received so much media attention, and these stories are a warning to other women who have thought about committing similar acts. The media is the tool used to restore social order.

## VICIOUS WIFE: BETTY BRODERICK

On the morning of November 5, 1989, Elisabeth "Betty" Broderick drove to her ex-husband's house where he was living with his new wife. Dan Broderick and Linda Kolkena lay sleeping as Betty quietly let herself into their house, crept up the stairs to their bedroom, and fired five shots at them, killing them both. She said she intended to go to Dan's home with the gun to kill herself in front of him, to show him how much he had hurt her, but the gun accidentally went off and she killed Dan and Linda instead.

Betty claimed that she was a victim of years of emotional abuse and a bitter divorce. She and Dan had been married for fourteen years. Betty helped put Dan first through Cornell Medical School, then Harvard Law School. Dan eventually became a successful at-torney in San Diego and she was a busy homemaker raising their four children. But as the years passed, the marriage began to sour. Dan had hired a young assistant, Linda Kolkena Broderick, to help him with his booming malpractice law firm. Betty began to accuse Dan of having an affair with Linda, but he responded by saying that it wasn't true. When Betty eventually discovered what she had feared about Dan and Linda, she went home, ripped up Dan's clothes, and made a bonfire with them in the backyard. In 1985, Betty and Dan separated and began a bitter divorce battle that did not end until 1988. Seven months after the divorce, Dan married Linda. Betty was enraged. She felt humiliated and betrayed, and lashed out at Dan, leaving menacing messages on his answering machine, throwing bottles through the windows of his home, and bad-mouthing him every chance she got. Her behavior change was noticeable to her friends; she grew increasingly neurotic as she saw the life she helped build slip away from her. Her behavior was growing increasingly violent toward Dan, so he filed for a restraining order (Geringer, 2001; Stumbo, 1993).

After Betty shot Dan and Linda Broderick, she turned herself in to police the next day. She was charged with their murders and went to trial. Court TV online has an episode devoted to the trial titled "California v. Broderick. Betty Broderick on Trial: Victim or Criminal?" On December 10, 1991, Betty Broderick was found guilty of two counts of second-degree murder for the deaths of Dan and Linda Broderick. She was sentenced to thirty-two years to life in prison (Geringer, 2001; Stumbo 1993).

Betty Broderick represents the unstable, emotional wife who did the unthinkable to her husband. Between 1976 and 1997, of the 60,000 murders women committed, more than 60 percent of them were against intimate partners or family members (Greenfeld & Snell, 1999). In 1998, murders by spouses were 53 percent of all intimate-partner homicides (Rennison & Welchans, 2000). Based on media coverage, the public has a perception that wives kill their husbands more frequently. Court TV covered *Nevada v. Rudin*, "The Black Widow Murder Trial." Margaret Rudin was accused of shooting her husband, Ron Rudin, in the head several times, burning his body to the point of nonrecognition, and dumping it in a ravine. Ron Rudin was a wealthy real estate tycoon who left 60 percent of his estate to Margaret in the event of his death. Sound fishy? Maybe. But was the trial deserving of eight hours of media coverage every day on Court TV for weeks? Certainly the only comparable media coverage of a wife killer in the twentieth century has been O.J. Simpson. However, one could argue that the reason for this was Simpson's fame and wealth. And he was acquitted.

In reality, female victims of homicide are more likely to be murdered by a husband, ex-husband, or boyfriend than male victims are likely to be killed by their wives, ex-wives, or girlfriends. Between

1976 and 1997, of the 400,000 murders committed by men, 20 percent of these were against an intimate partner or family member. So, in comparison, the 60 percent of the victims of female intimate murders equaled 36,000 fatalities, whereas the 20 percent of the victims of male intimate murders were 80,000 fatalities (Rennison & Welchans, 2000). In 1992 alone, approximately 12.8 percent of female victims of homicide (1,414 women) were known to have been killed by a husband, ex-husband, or boyfriend. In contrast, only 3 percent of the male victims of homicide (637 males) were killed by their wife, ex-wife, or girlfriend (Greenfeld & Snell, 2000; Bachman & Saltzman, 1995). In 1988, a large study was done by the Bureau of Justice Statistics on spouse-murder defendants in large urban counties, and it was discovered that "more husbands (20%) than wives (10%) had killed in a fit of jealousy over the mate's real or imagined infidelity" (Langan & Dawson, 1995, p. 3). In the same study, it was found that wives were the most frequent victims of fatal family violence. Eight thousand homicides were examined in this study, and a male was the assailant in about two-thirds of the family murders. Among the white murder victims, 38 percent of the victims were husbands and 62 percent were wives. In reading these statistics, we must always keep in mind the number correlation to the percentage. The accompanying table illustrates murder and manslaughter victim–offender relationships for 1991.

**PRISONERS WHO WERE INCARCERATED FOR VIOLENT OFFENSES**

| Inmate's Relationship to the Victim | Total No. of Prisoners | Total (%) | Murder (%) | Murder (No.) | Man-slaughter (%) | Man-slaughter (No.) |
|---|---|---|---|---|---|---|
| **Male prisoners who had:** | | | | | | |
| Intimate victims | 20,170 | 100 | 32 | 6,455 | 5 | 1,009 |
| Wives and ex-wives | 7,431 | 100 | 44 | 3,270 | 4 | 297 |
| Girlfriends | 12,739 | 100 | 25 | 3,185 | 6 | 764 |
| Total | 40,340 | | | 12,910 | | 2,070 |
| Total women killed | 55,320 | | | | | |
| **Female prisoners who had:** | | | | | | |
| Intimate victims | 2,345 | 100 | 61 | 1,430 | 16 | 375 |
| Husbands and ex-husbands | 1,308 | 100 | 73 | 955 | 10 | 131 |
| Boyfriends | 1,037 | 100 | 47 | 487 | 22 | 228 |
| Total | 4,690 | | | 2,872 | | 734 |
| Total men killed | 8,296 | | | | | |

Source: "Violence Between Intimates," table compiled from BJS Survey of Inmates in State Correctional Facilities, 1991 (Bachman & Saltzman, p. 8).

So what do all of these numbers mean? Men kill their wives, ex-wives, and intimate partners at a greater rate than women do. This does not reflect what the media reports to the public. In comparison to the "Black Widow" trials, how many "Bluebeard" trials have been reported and broadcast? Men have not been as criminalized as women when they have killed their mates. The entertainment industry doesn't make made-for-TV movies about men who kill their wives, either. Meredith Baxter Birney portrayed Betty Broderick in *Her Final Fury: Betty Broderick, the Last Chapter* (1992). This is just another example of the media sensationalizing this case. But all of this media coverage fails to report the facts: that among all homicide victims, women are particularly at risk for intimate and family killings. From 1976 to 1999, 62 percent of the victims of intimate homicides were women, while 38 percent were men. Of the offenders for those same years, men were 63.5 percent of the assailants in these intimate murders, and women made up only 36 percent (Fox & Zawitz, 2001).

## REBEL WIFE: LORENA BOBBITT

No name in the history of America has caused men to shudder as much as Lorena Bobbitt, who took a kitchen knife and cut off her husband John's penis while he slept. She then left the house, penis in hand, and drove around, eventually throwing the penis in a field. The penis was found and reattached to John, and Lorena was charged with malicious wounding for dismembering John. She claimed that she attacked him after he had raped her, and her defense was temporary insanity and self-defense at the time of the crime. On January 21, 1994, Lorena was found not guilty by reason of insanity and committed to a mental health facility for forty-five days for observation.

Lorena and John's marriage was far from perfect; they fought continuously, and on several occasions police were called to diffuse disputes. On June 21, 1992, Lorena filed for a restraining order against her husband, but failed to go through with it when she found out she had to appear in front of a judge. Two days later, Lorena took the law into her own hands and mutilated her allegedly abusive husband (Dershowitz, 1994). Despite the prevalence of domestic violence, female victims of it become criminalized when they "fight back." Marital rape occurs more frequently than the public is aware, but it has received little attention by the criminal justice system and our society. Some researchers have compared the psychological effects of being raped by one's intimate partner as being just as or even more devastating than other acts of violence. Victims are more likely to experience multiple assaults, completed sexual acts, and rape by someone they love and trust. Short-term effects of marital rape include anxiety, shock, intense fear, depression, suicidal ideation, and post-traumatic stress disorder. Women report higher rates of anger and depression when an intimate partner has raped them. Victims are less likely to report their assaults because of the relationship with the offender. Marital rape may be even more traumatic than stranger rape because the woman lives with her attacker and may live in constant fear of when another assault will occur (Bergen, 1999).

The media dismissed Lorena's claim of abuse and marital rape. The criminal justice system did too; John Bobbitt was acquitted of the charge. Lorena might have taken extreme measures against John, but the reality of domestic violence, aggravated assaults, and marital rape involving male offenders and female victims is disturbing. For both fatal and nonfatal violence, women are at higher risk than men of being victimized and injured by an intimate partner (Bachman & Saltzman, 1995; Craven, 1996). Fifty-two percent of female victims of intimate violence sustained an injury, and 41 percent required medical care (Craven, 1996, p. 3). In the *Sourcebook of Criminal Justice Statistics Online*, victim and offender relationships in personal victimization were as shown in the accompanying table for 1999.

| Relationship of Victim to Offender | Violent Crime | | Rape/Sex Assault | | Aggravated Assault | |
|---|---|---|---|---|---|---|
| | Number | Percent | Number | Percent | Number | Percent |
| All victims, total | 7,357,060 | 100 | 383,170 | 100 | 1,503,280 | 100 |
| Male victims, total | 4,016,580 | 100 | 39,340 | 100 | 944,720 | 100 |
| Intimate | 109,450 | 3 | 0 | — | 31,820 | 3 |
| Female victims, | 3,380,480 | 100 | 543,830 | 100 | 558,550 | 100 |
| total Intimate | 670,590 | 20 | 77,170 | 22 | 88,390 | 16 |

Source: Bureau of Justice Statistics, *Criminal Victimization 1999: Changes 1998–99 with Trends 1993–99* (online)

Husbands do not suffer injuries from domestic violence as wives do, although the Bobbitt case would make us believe differently. John Bobbitt sustained a heinous wound at the hands of Lorena, yet we do not hear of the tens of thousands of cases in which wives are injured and hospitalized due to intimate partner violence. Between 1993 and 1998, women made up an average total of 937,490 victims annually of intimate partner violence, as opposed to an average of 144,620 men during that same time period. Shockingly, an average 471,110 women annually were injured as a result of this domestic violence. Only 47,000 men were injured in those same five years (Rennison & Welchans, 2000, p. 3). It has been shown that women experience six to ten times more intimate violence than men (p. 3).

So what was the big deal with Lorena? She was an example of the "growing justification for vigilante violence by those who claim they cannot receive justice from the legal system" (Dershowitz, p. 3). She cut off the symbol of a man's power; silently, men cringed, and outwardly, women cheered. No other case of intimate partner violence has received so much media attention or created so many jokes. Locals refer to the city in which the crime occurred as "the place where men now sleep on their stomachs."

Court TV's episode "Assault, Revenge, or Self-Defense? The Trial of Lorena Bobbitt" takes the public through the history and trial of Lorena, but sadly, there was no movie deal for her. Actually, John Bobbitt came out pretty well through this ordeal. He appeared on numerous talk shows and television news magazines, and he went on to make a few adult movies. *John Wayne Bobbitt Uncut* came out in 1994, and *Frankenpenis* followed two years later. He also worked in a Nevada brothel for some time. The media made John Bobbitt a star because he survived his wife's attack, but has failed to give attention to the thousands of women who have endured years of domestic violence and have emerged triumphant. The only time these women are acknowledged are when they cut off their husband's penis, or worse yet, kill him.

## MONSTROUS MOTHER: SUSAN SMITH

It was every mother's nightmare: Someone had kidnapped her children. Susan Smith told Union County deputies that a black man had forced her from her car and driven off with her two screaming sons, three-year-old Michael and fourteen-month-old Alex. After the incident occurred, Smith ran to a nearby house and hysterically screamed that her children had been kidnapped. This launched a massive search to locate the boys, involving the Union County sheriff's department, the FBI, and SLED agents. The story soon became national news, and during the nine days of the boys' disappearance, Susan and David Smith appeared several times on national television, tearfully imploring the kidnapper to return their children (Eftimiades, 1995; Henderson & Fields, 1994).

On November 4, 1994, the search came to a close. Susan Smith admitted to killing her two children by letting her car roll into John D. Long Lake with the two boys strapped in their car seats in the backseat. Union County Sheriff Howard Wells held a press conference and announced, "Susan Smith has been arrested and charged with two counts of murder in connection with her children, Michael, 3, and Alexander, 14 months." A large gasp rose from the crowd (Henderson & Fields, 1994).

That gasp was echoed throughout America. How could a mother kill her own children? This is the worst crime a woman could commit. To add to public disgust was the fact that America had seen Susan Smith on television, blatantly lying to the public for nine days about the circumstances surrounding the disappearance of her children while a massive search was conducted. All along, Susan knew where to look.

As the story unfolded, several aspects seemed to contribute to the reason why Susan took the lives of her two sons. Susan and David Smith had separated after a rocky, troubled marriage, and Susan was having more frequent periods of depression. At the time of the drowning, Susan claimed that she wanted to commit suicide, but she couldn't bear the thought of her two sons growing up without a mother, so she would end their lives with hers. She felt that her whole life was wrong and she could not escape the loneliness, isolation, and failure that plagued her. She also revealed that she was in love with a man who didn't want a ready-made family. In everyone's opinion, this was the real motive for Susan to kill her children. Susan claimed that after she watched the car roll into the lake, she was overcome with what she had done to her children and desperately wanted to undo it. When she ran to the nearby house in hysterics, she formed her alibi.

At her trial, the prosecution asserted that Susan Smith wanted to escape her loneliness, unhappiness, and stresses in her life by establishing an exciting, intimate relationship with her wealthy boyfriend. In order to live this new life, Susan would need to free herself of her children and the demands of motherhood. The defense painted a different picture of Susan, one of a fragile woman who was the victim of an abusive past and whose emotional problems caused her to kill her sons. The jury didn't buy it, and they returned in two and a half hours with a guilty verdict of two counts of murder (Eftimiades, 1995; Pergament, 2001).

This was truly a case that became notorious because of the gender of the offender and her relationship to the victims. The media fails to cover stories in which fathers kill their children. In actuality, of all the children murdered from 1976 to 1999 who were under the age of five, 31 percent were killed by fathers and 30 percent were killed by mothers (Fox & Zawitz, 2004; Greenfeld, 1996). "Between 1976 and 1997, parents and stepparents murdered nearly 11,000 children. Mothers were responsible for a higher share of children killed during infancy, while fathers were more likely to have been responsible for the murders of children age 8 or older" (Greenfeld, 1996, p. 4). According to the Bureau of Justice Statistics' infanticide trends, "the number of homicides of children under age 5 has increased, but the rates have stayed the same" (Fox & Zawitz, 2004, p. 1). It was also revealed that from 1976 to 1999, "most of the children killed are male and most of the offenders are male" (Fox & Zawitz, 2004, p. 2). The first part of the statement rings true for the Smith case, but the second does not. The most common gender combination of victim and offender is male on male; then male on female, female on male, and the most uncommon combination of female on female. The father kills his children, regardless of gender, more frequently than the mother. The percentages of homicide type by gender from 1976 to 1999 show that men (both fathers and male acquaintances) have committed 61.1 percent of infanticides, while women (mothers and female acquaintances) have committed only 38.9 percent of them. Even so, whenever infanticide is discussed, the focus is almost always on a mother killing her child.

So why do we know names like Susan Smith, Darlie Routier, Alice Cummins, Diane Downs, and Melissa Drexler ("The Prom Mom")? All are women who have killed their children, and the media have taken this "depraved, immoral" crime and sensationalized it. Even though the percentage of mothers and fathers who kill their children is relatively the same, there are few or no Court TV episodes or *American Justice* programs that cover stories of fathers killing their children. The A&E network filmed a documentary about Susan Smith entitled "The Susan Smith Story: A Mother's Confession." The blurb that described the program reads, "Explore the true details of the tabloid case that riveted—and disgusted—America."

## CHILD SEDUCER: MARY KAY LETOURNEAU

It was a case that few could believe: a thirty-five-year-old woman had been accused of having a sexual relationship with a thirteen-year-old boy. The relationship between Mary Kay Letourneau and Vili Falaau began when he was a student in her sixth-grade class. They developed a mentor–friendship type of relationship that eventually turned more intimate. Mary Kay and Vili had sex when he was in seventh grade. Mary Kay's husband, Steve, became suspicious of the relationship and eventually discovered love letters Mary Kay had written to Vili. He contacted Washington Child Protective Services, and Mary Kay was arrested in the parking lot of the elementary school where she taught. At the time of her arrest, she was pregnant with Vili's baby. He was going to be a father at the age of fourteen. When the media broadcast the story of this affair, people were shocked and intrigued. Torrid details were made available to the public, and nothing was left to the imagination as Mary Kay was beginning to show signs of her pregnancy. It is interesting to note the media always followed Mary Kay's name with the statement that she was a "wife and mother of four children," as if saying that what she had done had caused her to abandon those roles.

On August 7, 1997, Mary Kay pleaded guilty to two counts of second-degree child rape, and was back in the courtroom on November 14 for sentencing. Court TV aired the hearing live. We saw a shaken Mary Kay Letourneau say what everyone wanted to hear: "I did something that I had no right to do, morally or legally. It was wrong and I am sorry." Then she dramatically ended her statement with, "It will not happen again. Please help me . . . help us all" (Noe, 2005). She was sentenced to six months in jail and three months of counseling for sex offenders. The judge warned Mary Kay to stay away from Vili, and if she violated the conditions of her sentence, she would be sentenced to seven years in prison. This did not thwart Mary Kay. Three months after her release, a police officer investigated a parked car in the early hours of the morning. He recognized Mary Kay Letourneau and assumed that the teenage boy in the passenger seat was the child she had been forbidden to contact. She was arrested and sent to prison, pregnant with Vili's second child. From the beginning, Mary Kay has professed that they were in love, and has viewed the laws against adult–child sexual relations as an obstacle keeping them from being together (Olsen, 1999).

Mary Kay Letourneau has been labeled "America's Most Famous Pedophile." Why is she so famous? Is it because she is the only pedophile in America? Certainly not. Is it because she is a woman? Absolutely. In his article, "Pedophiles and Child Molesters: The Slaughter of Innocence," Mark Gado (2001) states that Mary Kay is America's most famous female child molester: "Letourneau's case is rare. It does not seem to be part of the psychological composite of females to sexually molest a child. That compulsion, whatever its origin, seems to lie deep within the male psyche." So what are some names of "famous" male pedophiles? Have male pedophiles and child molesters had the same sort of media coverage as Mary Kay Letourneau? Where are the made-for-TV movies about men who molest children? Are there any that can compete with Penelope Ann Miller's sympathetic portrayal of Mary Kay in *The Mary Kay Letourneau Story: All-American Girl* (2000)?

There are people who support the relationship between the woman and the teenager. They say that they are in love, so why can't they be left alone? Would there be the same sentiment if a male teacher got a fourteen-year-old female student pregnant? Mary Kay Letourneau's story has been sensationalized and criminalized because she is a woman, even though this situation is a rare occurrence.

"Nearly all of the offenders in sexual assaults [of a child] reported to law enforcement were male (96%). Female offenders were most common in assaults against victims under age 6" (Snyder, 2000, p. 8). Based on a survey of inmates in state correctional facilities, only 3 percent of the offenders who committed violent crimes against children were female (Greenfield, 1996, p. 5). In 1991, only 3.4 percent of female offenders in state prisons had child victims; 96.6 percent of the male offenders had child victims (p. 5). A majority of the child victims are female. In the same study, 75.3 percent of the victims were girls, while 24.7 percent of them were boys. Also, nine out of ten of the offender–victim relationships were of the same race. Only 12.7 percent were of mixed-race combinations; Mary Kay Letourneau was Caucasian and Vili Falaau was Samoan.

All of the data supports the fact that this truly is a rare case. Men molest and rape children more than women do. But the media created a scandal with Mary Kay, perhaps because she was a female and did not fit the definition of a pedophile or child molester. However, some say that this makes Mary Kay the most dangerous of all child molesters, because she is someone we would least expect to molest a child.

There are two categories of child molesters: the situational child molester and the preferential child molester. Situational child molesters have sex with children for reasons that are not based in sexual desire. They do not prefer children as sexual partners but engage in sexual relations with them that are motivated by criminal factors. The victim is incidental and unimportant, and usually an incident will only occur once. Preferential child molesters have a sexual preference for children. They usually have a large number of victims and will seduce children, carrying their fantasies into reality (Gado, 2001).

Mary Kay is a one-boy woman. "In August 2004, Mary Kay Letourneau was released from prison after serving seven and a half years for raping a child. On May 21, 2005, Mary Kay Letourneau, 43, married Vili Falaau, now 22, in Woodinville, Washington, outside Seattle" (Noe, 2005). This seems to be the final chapter of a bizarre case with the "offender" and "victim" living happily ever after.

## FEMALE SERIAL KILLER: AILEEN WUORNOS

Aileen Wuornos has earned the title of "America's First Female Serial Killer." This could not be further from the truth. Female killers with multiple victims have been around long before Aileen, although these killers primarily focused on family members and the weapon of choice was poison. What makes Aileen different is that she killed strangers with a gun, and this sort of violence against strangers is more often associated with serial killers—male serial killers. Aileen is fundamentally different than all of the male serial killers the public is aware of, and these differences have somehow gotten lost in all of the hype surrounding her case.

Between 1989 and 1990, mysterious deaths were occurring along Interstates 75 and 95 in Florida. The bodies of men with multiple gunshot wounds were being found near the highways in wooded areas. Eventually, the bodies of seven men were discovered. Police were baffled as to the perpetrator and motive of these murders. There was evidence that the victims had been robbed, and almost always, the perpetrator left the scene in the victim's car (MacCleod, n.d.; Manners, 1995; Newton, 2000; Reynolds, 2004).

In an unrelated incident, witnesses saw a car accident in which the victims involved fled the scene after the event. Witnesses helped police draw up suspect sketches, and the media forced authorities to go public with the sketches on November 30, 1990. Tips poured in linking the sketches to two women, Tyria Moore and "Lee Blahovec." The two were traced through motel receipts, and detectives learned that "Blahovec's" real name was Aileen Wuornos. Meanwhile, Aileen was pawning items stolen from the murder victims and living a rootless lifestyle. She was picked up at a biker bar called "The Last Resort" for outstanding warrants under one of her aliases while they built a murder case against her (MacLeod, 2001).

With the help of her lover, Tyria Moore, police got a confession from Aileen on January 16, 1991. She said she was a prostitute who had been picked up by each victim for the purpose of having sex.

Soon the encounters became violent, and Aileen had no choice but to defend herself with the .22 caliber gun she had begun to carry for protection. She stated she murdered the seven men in self-defense "because I felt if I didn't shoot 'em and I didn't kill 'em, first of all . . . if they survived, my ass would be getting in trouble for attempted murder, so I'm up shit's creek on that one anyway, and if I didn't kill 'em, you know, of course, I mean I *had* to kill 'em . . . or, it's like retaliation, too. It's like, 'You bastards, you were going to hurt me' " (Newton, 2000, p. 244). "She was emphatic in her assertion that nothing was her fault, not the murders and not any circumstances that led her down the criminal path that was her life. Each victim had either assaulted her, threatened her, or raped her" (MacLeod, 2001).

Aileen's attorney engineered a plea bargain in which she would plead to six charges and receive six consecutive life terms. Aileen took the witness stand during her trial for the murder of Richard Mallory as the only defense witness, and her testimony proved to be devastating to her case. On January 27, 1992, the jury deliberated only two hours before returning with a verdict of guilty of first-degree murder. As she left the courtroom, Aileen exploded: "I'm innocent! I was raped! I hope you get raped! Scumbags of America!" On January 31, 1992 she was sentenced to die in the electric chair for the murder of Richard Mallory (Newton, 2000). Aileen did not go to trial for the other six murders. She pleaded no contest to the murders of Dick Humphreys, Troy Burress, and David Spears. She pleaded guilty to the murder of Charles Carskaddon in June 1992. This was her fifth death sentence. In early February 1993, she was sentenced to die after pleading guilty to the murder of Walter Gino Antonio. No charges were brought against her for the murder of Peter Siems, because his body was never found (MacLeod, n.d.).

Aileen Wuornos was executed on October 9, 2002, by lethal injection. Her last words were: "I'd just like to say I'm sailing with the Rock and I'll be back like Independence Day with Jesus, June 6, like the movie, big mothership and all. I'll be back" (MacLeod, n.d.).

There was no sexual fantasy component to these murders. Serial killers are driven by a sexual fantasy of control and/or torture of their victims, and there is almost always a sexual component to those murders. Granted, Aileen and her victim were in a sexual situation, but this was due to Aileen's employment, and there was no evidence of sexual assault on the victims by Aileen. Her motivation, she claims, was self-defense. In addition, there was a financial motivation because all of the victims had been robbed of anything of value. These murders cannot compare to their male counterparts; Aileen Wuornos is not even in the same league as Ted Bundy, John Wayne Gacy, or Jeffrey Dahmer.

A study was done involving 130 people working as prostitutes in the San Francisco area regarding the extent of violence in their lives.

> As adults in prostitution, 82% had been physically assaulted; 83% had been threatened with a weapon; and 68% had been raped while working as prostitutes. Of the 82% who had been physically assaulted, customers had assaulted 55% of the victims. Eighty-eight percent had been physically threatened while in prostitution. Of the 68% who had been raped while working as prostitutes, 48% reported being raped more than five times. Forty-six percent of those who reported being raped stated they had been raped by customers. (Farley & Barkan, 2001)

This one study makes us wonder if Aileen's claims were true, but as a society we tend to view prostitutes as lower-class citizens who choose to work in a profession in which they don't mind the risks. No woman wants to be victimized, and unfortunately, prostitution is a high-risk occupation in which victimization occurs at an alarming rate. So why do we roll our eyes when Aileen claims that she killed in self-defense? We would certainly feel differently if she were a homemaker or held a "dignified" job.

Males are more likely than females to be victimized by a stranger. They are about as likely to be victimized by a stranger (49 percent) as by someone they know (51 percent) (Craven, 1996). In "Women Offenders," Lawrence Greenfeld (Greenfeld & Snell, 2000) states that "violent offenders most often victimized persons of the same gender. More than 3 out of 4 female offenders had a female victim; about 7 out of 10 males had a male victim. About 29 percent of violent offenders had a victim of a different gender; 9 out of 10 of these offenders were males with female victims. Overall, female-to-female violence accounted for 11 percent of all violent offenders, and only 3% of violent offenders were women who attacked males" (p. 3).

So what does this tell us? That once again, this case is rare. Between 1976 and 1999, only 6.7 percent of female offenders were involved in sex-related homicides; 93.3 percent of the perpetrators of these crimes were men (Fox & Zawitz, 2004, p. 2). In 1995, the FBI's Uniform Crime Reporting System reported that females represented 23 percent of all known homicide victims in the United States. In single-victim–single-offender incidents, males are more likely to be slain by males (89 percent). Similarly, nine out of ten female victims were killed by males (Craven, p. 2). Statistics for female violent offenders who had male victims were difficult to find. There are numerous numbers and percentages in relation to the victim–offender relationship as being strangers, but there is no evidence to suggest the gender of the offender. This lack of information only supports the rarity of the occurrences. In relation to homicide in general, men offend at a higher rate (87.8 percent) than women (12.2 percent) and are more often victims of homicide than women (76.4 percent compared to 23.6 percent). Also, concerning multiple victims, 93.7 percent were male offenders, while only 6.3 percent were female (Fox & Zawitz, p. 2). Aileen is part of the 6.3 percent of female offenders who had multiple victims, an incredibly small percentage over the span of twenty-three years.

Even so, the media created a monster. Companies clamored for book deals and movie rights. Jean Smart portrayed Aileen in the made-for-TV movie *Overkill: The Aileen Wuornos Story*. This is yet another example of the media taking a rare incident and sensationalizing it, thus causing the public to think that it is a regular occurrence. Aileen was targeted because she was a woman, and women who kill several strangers are truly rare. She was also a prostitute and a lesbian, two aspects of her life that made her more deviant in society's eyes and clashed with the socially constructed role that women should fill of the puritanical heterosexual wife and/or mother.

There is no question that these cases, as well as many other well-known cases in which the woman is the offender, are sensationalized by the media even though their occurrences are rare. Particularly in the cases of Lorena Bobbitt, Mary Kay Letourneau, and Aileen Wuornos, they are the first of their kind. This does not mean that there is an upward increase of female offending; that is merely an illusion created by the media. I suppose that society has the view that men commit crime all the time, so stories about male wife killers, child killers, wife beaters, child molesters, and serial killers occur so often that they have become commonplace and mundane. Women who commit these crimes are rarities, or cause such tremendous moral outrage in society because they have gone against the cultural values that society has placed on women and female roles. This is the stuff that gets ratings. This is the stuff of made-for-TV movies.

Roslyn Muraskin was interviewed on television regarding Aileen Wuornos. Throughout the interview it was insisted that Aileen Wuornos was the first female serial killer and though Muraskin objected, there was no convincing the moderator. The show has been repeated over and over on television at all hours and over these many years since Wuornos's execution. Obviously, Wuornos made headlines, and headlines are still being made.

## DISCUSSION QUESTIONS

1. What is it about women criminals that attracts so much media attention?

2. A teacher and a student have sex and she has children. What is the fascination of such a story to the media?

3. Are female pedophiles so much more interesting than male pedophiles that the media plays it up as it does? Explain.

4. What was it about Aileen Wuornos that attracted so much media attention when there were approximately sixty-two known female serial killers before her?

5. Is the media capable of creating female monsters who kill their children and abuse their loved ones, or is it done because females in crime are so rare?

# 18

# Martha Stewart

## *This Case Is About Lying*

An Associated Press story, dated Friday, December 31, 2004, reported that "Martha Stewart, who built a billion-dollar media empire based on her holiday and home decorating tips, was unable to lead her team to victory in a prison decoration contest." Stewart, along with her fellow inmates at "a federal prison camp in Alderson, West Virginia, crafted paper cranes to be hung from the ceiling. . . . They lost out to a competing team that built a nativity scene showing 'pictures of snow-covered hills and sleds and clouds on the wall.'" Each prison team was given $25 worth of ribbons, construction paper, glitter, and glue to build some sort of display with the theme "Peace on Earth." Why is this newsworthy?

Martha Stewart had been convicted, along with her stockbroker, for having lied about unloading shares of stock in ImClone Systems, Inc. before the price plummeted in 2001. The headlines read, "Martha Indicted, Resigns." CNN/Money (Ulick, 2003) reported that "Martha Stewart resigned Wednesday as chairman and CEO of the company she founded, just hours after a federal indictment accused her and her former stockbroker of lying to investigators who were probing her profitable sale of ImClone Systems stock." By a nine-count, forty-one-page indictment of Stewart, a picture was painted of a cover-up in which "Stewart and her former broker at Merrill Lynch, Peter Bacanovic, obstructed justice and made false statements."

According to the FBI this criminal case was about lying: lying to the FBI, lying to the SEC, and lying to investors. Stewart had entered federal court in Manhattan and had surrendered herself to federal authorities. At her nine-minute arraignment, she pleaded not guilty.

"The indictment comes a year after it was revealed that Stewart in late 2001 sold 3,928 ImClone shares a day before a regulatory setback sent the stock tumbling" (Ulick). What had to be determined was whether Stewart, who was a friend of ImClone's then-CEO Samuel Waksal, knew beforehand of the sale that had netted her, a multimillionaire, about $229,000. Stewart was charged with two counts of making false statements. She faced charges of obstructing justice regarding her own company, Martha Stewart Living Omnimedia, where she was charged with defrauding investors by falsely inflating stock prices. Her own attorneys seized on the absence of insider trader charges, which were the focus of considerable speculation.

Stewart is one of the nation's wealthiest persons because she took Living Omnimedia public in October 1999. A guilty conviction on all the counts would have given Stewart up to thirty years in prison.

It was Stewart's contention that she had "an agreement with her broker to sell the shares when they fell below $60. But both the SEC's suit and the indictment dispute that contention, saying Stewart sold the shares after learning that Waksal, who left ImClone last year, was trying to unload his stock. [Allegedly] . . . by selling when she did, Stewart avoided losses of $45,673" (Ulick). Interestingly, this was a very minimal profit for Stewart, who in the years 2000 and 2001 had been named on *Forbes* magazine's list of the 400 wealthiest Americans.

All kinds of questions were posed both in the courts and by the press: "Are the charges being filed because the Department of Justice is attempting to divert the public's attention from its failure to charge the politically connected managers of Enron and WorldCom who may have fleeced the public out of billions of dollars?" Had the government brought this particular case "because (Stewart) is a woman who has successfully competed in a man's business world by virtue of her talent, hard work, and demanding standards" (Ulick)?

A poll was taken on an informal Web site where a majority of the 64,000 readers indicated that the government *was not* being too harsh on Stewart. Trial by your peers on a Web site?

In an interview by Jeffrey Toobin, CNN's legal correspondent, as reported in *The New Yorker* magazine, the feeling was that the government had a strong case, because if not and it lost, it would be very embarrassing.

CNNMoney reported: "As she faces possible jail time, Martha Stewart invoked the name of Nelson Mandela, South Africa's persecuted anti-apartheid hero, saying 'many, many good people have gone to prison' " (Crawford, 2004).

> Her declaration came in a TV interview taped two hours after the homemaking diva was sentenced to five months in prison and two years' probation Friday for lying to investigators about her sale of ImClone Systems stock in late 2001.
>
> Federal Judge Miriam Goldman Cedarbaum also ordered Stewart to serve five months of home confinement after her release and fined the lifestyle expert $30,000.
>
> The sentence was the minimum the judge could impose under federal sentencing guidelines. The fine, while relatively small given Stewart's wealth, was the maximum allowed under federal rules. (Crawford)

An appeal was to be heard but was stopped by Stewart.

In an interview by Barbara Walters on ABC's *20/20,* Stewart was asked "how she would cope with prison life, including strip searches. . . . [Stewart's answer was] I could do it . . . I'm a really good camper. I can sleep on the ground. . . . There are many, many good people who have gone to prison . . . look at Nelson Mandela."

Mandela had been imprisoned for 27 years before rising to become a leader of the African National Congress.

"Stewart, who had been steadfast in proclaiming her innocence, told Walters, 'I didn't cheat the little people. . . . We're all little people. I didn't cheat anybody out of anything.'"

Stewart's reaction to the sentence was that, though disappointed she was to serve prison time, it was fair. She had asked the judge to "consider all the good that I have done, all the contributions I have made and all the intense suffering that has accompanied every single moment of the past two and one half years," but prison time was to be given, though only five months. She had indicated in her televised interview with Walters that she had hoped at the very least for some community service, but it could have been worse.

The news media reported further that Stewart was angry about the two-year legal drama and that many people had lost their jobs as a result of the investigation. She indicated that she had lost her CEO position at Martha Stewart Omnimedia and that she was angered and saddened by such action.

The Stewart case was one of a number of criminal indictments against corporate executives. "While comparatively small in terms of the dollars at stake and the gravity of the crime, Stewart's obstruction of justice case has been a powerful public relations vehicle for government officials to send the broad message that *corporate malfeasance* will not be tolerated" (Walters). It was continually pointed out by her supporters that Stewart had been singled out because of her high profile.

Her statement before sentencing, as reported by the media: "I seek the opportunity to repair the damage wrought by the situation, to get on with what I have always thought was a good, worthwhile and exemplary life. My hopes that my life will not be completely destroyed lie entirely in your competent and experienced and merciful hands. Thank you and peace be with you."

After sentencing, Martha reacted by stating it was a shameful day. "What was a small personal matter became, over the last two years, an almost fatal circus of unprecedented proportion. I have been choked and almost suffocated to death. I'll be back." And, of course, she is today.

Then the headlines read, "Martha Stewart Found Guilty." Stories were headlined "How Martha Ended Up in Court." Polls were taken by the media before sentencing:

### What Should Be Martha Stewart's Punishment?

Community service

Community service and a fine

Jail time and a fine

Fine

Jail time

I don't know

None of the above

*Vote now!*

The media had a heyday with this story. Headlines read: "One Inmate's Experience at Alderson"; "Martha Stewart Counts Her Chickens"; "Martha and the Mandelas"; "Martha's Fall from Grace"; "Martha Stewart Found Guilty"; "Martha Trial: 'A Conspiracy of Dunces'"; "Martha Trial: 'It Makes No Sense'"; "Martha Trial: Count 9 Stuck in Judge's Craw"; "Martha Trial: Tales from Beyond the Court." When Martha was indicted, the headlines read, "Martha's Goose on Slow Burn"; when the trial began, the headlines read, "Martha's Defense Gets Weird." During the testimony the headlines read "Martha Trial: Everyone Is Telling the Same Story"; "Martha Trial: Recovered Trash"; "Martha Trial: She Won't Testify"; "Martha Trial: No Specific Recollection."

From Forbes.com came the headline "Martha's Little Lies." Elizabeth MacDonald reported on February 4, 2004, "While she isn't charged with insider trading, it's the tiniest—and seemingly silliest—of lies that could hurt Martha Stewart. As events at the trial unfold, we've put together a roadmap of the alleged lies. With our doubt-o-meter, we've also handicapped both the prosecution's and the defense's success in eliciting reasonable doubt in the jury on the major issues at stake." Doubt-o-meters were put on Web sites so the readers could prejudge Stewart.

Cartoons were drawn. One was a picture of a prison and someone asking, "So I wonder who's moving in next door?" The next cell was decorated with curtains and flowers. Other cartoons showed regular cells with bars and others with curtains and trellis work.

While incarcerated, Martha Stewart remained very much the lady. From her Web site, www.marthatalks.com, she wrote the following letter to her friends.

Dear Friends:

> When one is incarcerated with 1,200 other inmates, it is hard to be selfish at Christmas—hard to think of Christmases past and Christmases future—that I know will be as they always were for me: beautiful. So many of the women here in Alderson will never have the joy and well-being that you and I experience. Many of them have been here for years—devoid of care, devoid of love, devoid of family.

> I beseech you all to think about these women—to encourage the American people to ask for reforms, both in sentencing guidelines, in length of incarceration for nonviolent first offenders, and for those involved in drug-taking. They would be much better served in a true rehabilitation center than in prison where there is no real help, no real programs to rehabilitate, no programs to educate, no way to be prepared for life "out there" where each person will ultimately find herself, with no skills and no preparation for living.

> I am fine, really. I look forward to being home, to getting back to my valuable work, to creating, cooking, and making television. I have had time to think, time to write, time to exercise, time to not eat the bad food, and time to walk and contemplate the future. I've had my work here

too. Cleaning has been my job—washing, scrubbing, sweeping, vacuuming, raking leaves, and much more. But like everyone else here, I would rather be doing all of this in my home, and not here, away from family and friends.

I want to thank you again, and again, for your support and encouragement. You have been so terrific to me and to everyone who stood by me. I appreciate everything you have done, your emails, your letters, and your kind, kind words.

Happy Holidays.

Martha Stewart

Martha Stewart served her time, and next we heard stories of how Martha spent her time in jail.

As a postscript to the Martha Stewart saga, on the evening of July 5, 2005, on the 11 P.M. news, the headlines were: the stormy weather; the Olympics decision to be made the next day; and the fact that while in prison, Martha Stewart's nickname was M. Diddy. It was not until 11:29 that it was said that Stewart's prosecution was about bringing her down "to scare other people." This was reported as well the next morning by the Associated Press News, which summed up an interview given to *Vanity Fair* magazine, that she agreed with those "who say her crime—lying about a personal stock sale—is far different from massive corporate scandals such as Enron Corp., WorldCom. Inc, and Tyco International Ltd." Further on in this interview, Stewart claimed, "Bring 'em down a notch to scare other people. If Martha can be sent to jail, think hard before you sell that stock" (Associated Press, July 6, 2005).

She also complained about the electronic monitoring bracelet that she had to wear on her ankle after being released: "She has complained repeatedly that it irritates her skin—Stewart said she knew how to remove it. 'I watched them put it on. You can figure out how to get it off. . . . It's on the Internet. I looked it up'" (Associated Press, July 6, 2005).

However, Stewart took her house arrest seriously. She reported to her probation officer as required, and in fact, when she was two or three minutes late, she apologized.

A federal appeals court was considering her bid to overturn her conviction. Asked in the interview whether apologies were in order, her answer was simply that she was "sorry for the 'chaos' her prosecution caused but suggested that she was not personally to blame."

Is there something about being a celebrity that allows a person to be treated somewhat differently? Why does the media grab on to such stories? Do they sell much more than stories about the street criminal who kills, robs, attacks, and burglarizes? Apparently so.

## DISCUSSION QUESTIONS

1. There was a media blitz, an almost circus-like atmosphere surrounding the case of Martha Stewart. Why? What was the attraction to the media?

2. The stories described Martha's decorations in the prison where she served time. Why was this so newsworthy?

3. Was the Martha Stewart story an embarrassment, or was it worth all the media coverage? She did not kill anyone. What was it that made this so desirable a story?

4. Think of all the headlines about Martha Stewart the businesswoman. How would you write the story?

5. Did the media make Martha Stewart more of a success story than before?

# 19

# Can the Mass Media Do Good?

What can we say that is good about the media? According to Surette (1998):

- The mass media may help form attitudes toward new subjects where little prior opinion exists.
- The mass media may influence attitudes that are weakly held.
- The mass media may strengthen one attitude at the expense of a series of others when the strength of the several attitudes is evenly balanced.
- The mass media may suggest new courses of action that appear to better satisfy existing wants and needs.
- The mass media's strongest and most universally recognized effect remains the reinforcement or strengthening of existing dispositions and attitudes. (p. 200)

The mass media does have usefulness because it allows the public to know what is happening. The problems are when the media overdoes it by overemphasizing the bad or convicting the individuals who have yet to appear in court. "The repetitiveness and pervasiveness of the media's general crime-and-justice content increase the possibility that the media have significant unplanned effects, particularly in the area of crime and justice and especially for persons with limited alternative sources of information. And because of the media's content emphasis on law enforcement and predatory crime, it is expected any media reality efforts would promote crime control constructions more than due process" (Surette, p. 201).

What has been pointed out throughout this work by case examples and narrative is that the audience appears to judge a social concern as having importance to the extent that it is emphasized by the media. The media influences public policy "through a linear process: stories of an issue appear, the issue increases in importance to the public, the public becomes alarmed, interest groups mobilize, and policy makers respond." The influence of the media is not necessarily direct. "More often it is mediated through multiple steps and social networks and the acceptance of media-promulgated crime-and-justice claims by the public is an unresolved process." There lies the possibility that once the public has been convinced, then the media plays a role in reinforcing the opinions, and where there is disagreement, the media becomes unconvincing. If this is so, then "the greater match between the media and those who attend to the media more would be due not to the media's constructive influence on the public's agenda but to a selective exposure and retention of information on the part of the public" (Surette, p. 202).

The effects of the media vary. It is more common for the television to play a large role in convincing the population of what is occurring. Do the media play a role in policy making? "Research into the effects of investigative reporting has revealed that the most consistent factor in determining the impact of the media on policy is the relationship that forms between the media and local policy makers" (Surette, p. 202). The media has more than a minimal effect on the populace and on policy makers. Raising the public's fears about crime results in hype regarding public anxiety about crime, resulting in other serious problems, such as social problems like hunger, being kept off the public agenda.

In reviewing the literature, Surette (1998) has developed the following hypotheses:

- *Substitution:* Persons lacking alternative sources of knowledge substitute media information, which raises fear.
- *Resonance:* Persons with victim experience or knowledge focus on media information, which compounds preexisting fear.
- *Vulnerability:* Persons less able to prevent victimization are made more fearful by media information.
- *Affinity:* Persons who demographically resemble media victims are made more fearful by media information.
- *Ceiling effects:* Persons who already have high levels of fear are therefore beyond the media's influence. (p. 207)

Abstract danger legitimizes public surveillance and regimented personal action by forging the spectacle between the media, the audience, and comprehensive social control. The real power to control crime pales in comparison to the illusion of control and the universalized desire to control the "evil" that is inscribed in even the most insipid media accounts of crime. These tech-cultural rituals . . . —marching the accused person in handcuffs before a crew of reporters and cameras— feeds the desire for justice. The criminal is reduced to the glare of publicity, caught by the system of control that protects all of us. It is a compelling drama for the media to project to an audience eager to believe that the system of control works. The spectacle of reality produced by mass-media images reduces life, justice, and the real crime that exists to something less than the abstraction. (Potter & Kappeler 1998, p. 339)

Is there a relationship among crime, justice, public policy and the media? The research appears to suggest that the news media does affect policy. "The content of television news broadcasts favoring or opposed to specific policies consequently shifts public opinion in the same direction as the news coverage" (Surette, p. 213). The media plays a decisive role in the social construction of reality. The conclusion to be reached is that the media does alter reality, and affects how the audience views the criminal justice system. The media is responsible for molding reality. Surette refers to *media looping*. "In *media looping,* media content is extracted from one context or component of the media and reused and reframed in another. It is not unusual for looping to result in new, ambiguous media realities. These looping effects are observed in both real events that are mediated such as the Rodney King beating and the Oklahoma City bombing and in created-for-media pseudo-events found in shows like COPS" (p. 229).

The portrayal of crime by the mass media is assumed to distort the kind of crime that exists and the crimes being committed.

# 20

# If a Story Isn't Depicted by the Media, It Doesn't Exist

"No leads, no witnesses, no problem," a quote taken from Court TV's Crime Library, Criminal Minds and Methods (www.crimelibrary.com, 2004).

The leads continue:[1]

**Aum Cult**   A fascinating study of the religious terrorist cult that attracted some of Japan's brightest young people and created a billion dollars in assets, much of which was used to fund development of anthrax and other weapons of mass destruction.

**Nick Berg**   Bloodstain analysis from the video of his murder shows forensic irregularities that may cast doubt on events.

**Osama bin Laden**   The man who has declared a holy war against any nation, specifically America, he deems to be a threat to the nation of Islam. Now the most wanted man in the world, he continues to evade capture, promising to fight to the death for his ideology.

**Biological and Chemical Warfare Program**   Trial of Dr. Wouter Basson focuses on alleged attempts to use chemical and biological weapons on African rebels.

---

[1]All of these case headlines can be found in Court TV's Crime Library at www.crimelibrary.com.

**Ted Kaczynski**   The whole amazing story of the genius madman who was known as the Unabomber and how he escaped the death penalty.

**Eric Randolph**   Handsome, mysterious and very, very dangerous, he is the suspected bomber of the Atlanta Olympic Park, an abortion clinic, gay bar, and other terrorist bombings. Long the object of a global manhunt, Rudolph, a trained survivalist was recently caught.

**Tylenol Murders**   One of the first terrorist cases in the U.S. dealt with the poisoning of medicines. Tremendous investigative efforts and preventive techniques did not completely stop copycats from continuing the initial reign of terror.

**Aldrich Ames**   CIA spy who betrayed his country in a very major way. Expert Pete Earley tells the story of this very damaging spy and what may have motivated him.

**Christopher Boyce and Andrew Daulton Lee**   Two long-time friends go into the espionage business, selling spy satellite drawings to the Russians. One escapes from jail and starts a new life. This story was the basis of the movie and book, *The Falcon and the Snowman*.

**Bonnie and Clyde**   Romeo and Juliet in a getaway car.

**Sue Basso**   Depraved woman traps mentally handicapped man so she can use him as slave and kill him for insurance.

**Robert Blake**   The full story behind the murder of Bonnie Lee Bakley and the trial of her celebrity husband. New chapters track the highs and woes of the trial.

**Christian Brando**   Marlon Brando's son murders his pregnant, mentally disturbed sister's boyfriend in a drunken rage—a tragedy that keeps on playing long after the murder.

**T. Cullen Davis**   Billionaire oil man goes to trial for murdering his daughter and wife's boyfriend, shooting a witness, assaulting his wife, and paying to have a judge murdered: the best "justice money can buy."

**Michael Fletcher**   Psychopathic lawyer murders his pregnant wife, carries on with lady judge. Now updated to include his trial and sentencing.

**Marvin Gaye**   Marketed as Motown's lover man, he beat the women he loved. He sang of soulful romance, yet forced his wives into degrading sex. All this ended after he attacked his father, who then shot and killed him.

**Dr. Jeffrey MacDonald**   Did the Green Beret really kill his wife and two girls?

**Darlie Routier**   Was she one of the most heartless criminals in America—killing her two little boys—or a victim of an overbearing prosecution? An update to this mystery.

**Dr. Sam Sheppard**   Forty-eight years after the murder of Marilyn Sheppard and numerous trials, it looks as though the Energizer Bunny of murder cases has finally wound its way through the Ohio courts, but though the trials may be over, new murder suspects continue to emerge.

**Joel Steinberg**   "The Killing of Lisa" by Detective Mark Gado explores the monstrous abuse that a New York lawyer commits on his family and the nightmarish destruction of a promising woman executive by a brutal, drug-obsessed control freak.

**Angels of Death—The Female Nurses**   Nurses continue to murder their patients. Dr. Katherine Ramsland examines the motives and some high-profile and recent cases.

**Velma Barfield**   This adoring mother and pious Christian grandmother had a secret habit—she poisoned her husbands, boyfriends, elderly people in her care, and even her mother. The amazing thing is how long this Black Widow serial poisoner (since executed) got away with it.

**Martha Beck and Raymond Fernandez**   The story of a desperately lonely overweight woman who lets herself fall into partnership with a man who murders women for money. The so-called Lonely Hearts Murders, entwined in voodoo magic and kinky sex, became one of the most sensational cases of the 1940s.

**Mary Ann Cotton**   Murdered between 15 and 21 of her close relatives by arsenic poisoning. Why? For money, personal dislike, or they got in her way over something she wanted.

**Genene Jones**   Texas pediatric nurse takes over the care of babies and murders them by injecting one after another. Almost as criminal is how the hospitals and staff ignored the problem until Genene's shift became known as the Death Shift.

**Sylvia Likens**   Sixteen-year-old girl found murdered with "I'm a prostitute and proud of it," burned onto her stomach. Suspicion focused on the woman who cared for her.

**Ruth Snyder and Judd Gray**   The real story of lust, greed, and murder that inspired the great film-noir classic, *Double Indemnity, The Postman Always Rings Twice,* and *Body Heat.*

**Marybeth Tinning**  All nine of her babies died suddenly without any rational explanation—until she confessed.

**Carolyn Warmus**  Every married man who ever thought of cheating on his wife quaked when he saw Glenn Close as the maniacal girlfriend in the movie *Fatal Attraction*. In 1989, a real-life "Fatal Attraction" burst into the New York headlines targeting a combination of sex, obsession, and death. Attractive and sexy heiress Carolyn Warmus goes after her man and destroys everything in her way.

**The Dartmouth Murders**  Two very popular married Ivy League professors are brutally murdered by two young men from good families who murdered in order to steal money for a pipe dream.

**Amy Fisher**  Long Island "Lolita," or a mixed-up teenager under the thumb of an older man? Fisher is now married to a police officer. They have two children. She is a reporter for a local newspaper.

**Dr. Joseph Mengele**  Nazi death camp doctor specialized in horrible experiments on Jewish twin children.

**Live Fast, Die Young**  Francis Crowley, 19 years old and the face of a choirboy, created havoc wherever he went. His heart-pounding story inspired the Jimmy Cagney classic *White Heart*.

**Jonestown**  A reason to die; tragic deaths of the followers of the Jim Jones cult.

**Sabotage**  United Flight 629 explodes in the air outside Denver, killing 44 people. Intensive FBI investigation yields the murderer who sabotaged the plane.

**Richard Speck**  Famous murderer of the Chicago nurses.

**The Birdman of Alcatraz**  Robert Stroud, self-taught prison inmate, spent most of his adult life in jail becoming an expert on birds and their breeding and diseases. Stroud was a very controversial prisoner who fought until his death for the freedom to pursue his scientific achievements.

**Kitty Genovese Murder**  *A Cry in the Night,* the famous murder of a lovely young woman in New York City. Thirty-seven people witnessed it and did not want to get involved. Detective Mark Gado examines the mindset of these silent witnesses and the serial murderer responsible for Kitty's death.

**The Martha Moxley Murder**  The Martha Moxley murder trial culminates in a guilty verdict for Michael Skakel. Read the facts leading up to this historical decision.

**Edgar Allan Poe**   Master of the horror story, father of the detective whodunit, and famous American poet died suddenly. Everyone assumed that he drank himself to death, but the facts of the case point to murder.

**William Desmond Taylor**   One of Hollywood's most successful directors is murdered. A studio executive goes through his house searching for evidence of scandal, plants monogrammed underwear with a famous actress's initials. What is the studio trying to hide? Who of the many suspects had a motive for murder?

**Career Girl Murders**   The savage sex-murders of two girls on Manhattan's Upper East Side shocked even the most hardened investigators. The case served as the blueprint for a popular television show, *Kojak*. It was one man's incredible odyssey through the Kafka-like maze of New York City courts that undermined the sacred concept of American justice and shattered the credibility of the nation's largest police force.

Crime headlines are alive and very much with us, as can be seen by the preceding examples. Hollywood and made-for-television movies have capitalized on the headlines of yesterday and today. Though crime statistics are down, the reporting of crime is not. Our correctional facilities are loaded with criminals locked up for longer periods of time than ever before. How accurate is crime reporting? Only as accurate as the reporter reporting the facts, and only as accurate as needed for the ratings. As long as ratings are involved and needed, as long as competition in television broadcasting exists, there will always be discrepancies in the reporting of crime. Headlines sell! What drives the public's interest in a crime story? The facts or the headlines?

Crime will always be part of our life; larger or smaller statistics will exist, but crime will always be there. This work presents questions to be considered and discussed. There are no easy answers as to how to present criminal acts. Today's technology does not help present criminal acts in an easy fashion. Who makes the headlines, the media or the criminal? The answer is not easy, but it would appear that the media plays a very large role in what we see and what we read.

# 21

# Conclusion

As previously stated, crime headlines are alive and very much with us, as can be seen by the examples identified throughout this work. Hollywood and made-for-television movies have capitalized on the headlines of yesterday and today. The reporting of crime events is very evident in the daily news on television, radio, and in newspapers. Though crime statistics are down, the reporting of crime is not. Our correctional facilities are overloaded with criminals locked up for longer periods of time than ever before. How accurate is crime reporting? Only as accurate as the reporter reporting the facts, and only as accurate as needed for the ratings. As long as ratings are involved and needed, as long as the competition in television broadcasting exists, there will always be discrepancies in the reporting of crime. Headlines sell! What drives the public's interest in a crime story? The facts or the headlines?

The media's impact on crime is evident. There is tremendous interaction between the media and crime itself. The media affects our judgment, our attitudes, our perceptions of crime, and societal reaction to crime in general. Certainly, as we have seen, the portrayal of crime by the media is a distortion of the facts, or in any event, it presents the facts as the media views it. There will always be room for sensational headlines, for those stories that appeal to the inner emotions of the readership or of those watching the news or going to the movies. The reporting of crime by the media has as its main purpose  selling newspapers, getting the best ratings, and bringing the populace into the theatres while making claim to true reporting. Is there a filtering process that takes place, or is the populace truly taken in by the media? As viewed by Potter and Kappeler, "[t]he real power to control crime pales in comparison to the illusion of control and universalized desire to control the 'evil' that is inscribed in even the most insipid media accounts of crime" (p. 339).

Our desire to see justice is when the perpetrator is viewed in handcuffs being led away by law enforcement officers regardless of his or her guilt or innocence. That one picture tells it all, guilt by association, guilt by the media. If it is not so, then why would it be viewed by an audience?

Surette (1992) states, "We have been conditioned to receive the entertainment and knowledge the media provide without considering where this entertainment and knowledge come from, what effect they have on our attitudes and perceptions, and how they affect society" (p. ix). If people believe what they read and see, then we have a criminal justice system that in and of itself speaks only of sensationalism and not of justice for all.

The public's knowledge of crime is fundamentally derived from the media. This includes our fear of crime. We have a certain fascination with crime. It is the mass media that plays a significant role in the interpretation of criminality and our criminal justice system. From our research, we see a connection between fear of crime and the attitudes of criminal justice policies. Crime, as it is depicted in the media, is much more violent, random, and dangerous than crime is by and of itself. The larger amount of articles, shows, and pictures depicting crime, the more fear is instilled in the populace, particularly in those areas that have higher crime rates than others. The portrayal by the media of crime incidents and the hype by the media has been found to be significantly related to our fear of crime, of being raped, beaten, robbed, having our homes burglarized, being carjacked, and getting killed.

As depicted by the media, the fear of crime is inextricably connected to the pressure by the public to solve crime. If the media portrays law enforcement officers as incompetent and unable to solve crimes, then the fear of victimization grows in large proportion. There appears to be, according to some researchers, an overdramatization of crime in society. The actual fear of crime may be the impetus for tougher policies such as "three strikes and you're out." By reading about crime on a daily basis, by viewing crime shows on television, by watching crime as depicted in the movies, we have a stereotyped view of crime and of those who commit crime. By inaccurately presenting crime, by overemphasizing the kind of headlines we see on a daily basis, the media has won.

We conclude thusly: We have only to speculate that the knowledge of crime by the media is formed through media consumption. Crime will always be part of our lives, larger or smaller statistics will exist, but crime will always be there. What this work does is present questions to be contemplated and discussed. There are no easy answers as to how to present criminal acts, and today's technology does not help present criminal acts in an easy fashion. Who makes the headlines? The media or the criminal? The answer is not easy, but it would appear that the media plays a very large role in what we see and what we read. The media itself may play a prominent role in crime and the kinds of solutions we seek.

# References

Ackman, D. (2004, March 5). Martha Stewart found guilty. *Forbes.com*. Retrieved from www.forbes.com/2004/03/05ex_da_0305marthafinal_print.html.

Allen, C. (2003, March 17). Welcome home: Abducteen coping well. *Psychology Today*. Retrieved from www.psychologytoday.com/articles/pto-20030317-000001.html

Allen, C. (2003, March 18). More on the Elizabeth Smart Case. *Psychology Today*. Retrieved from http://www.psychologytoday.com/articles/pto-20030318-000003.html

Answers.com (n.d.). Retrieved from www.answers.com/topic/elizabeth-smart-kidnapping.

Associated Press (2003, March 14). Quoting from Officer Bill O'Neal concerning Elizabeth Smart.

———. (2003, November 21). Jackson clashed 10 years ago. *Newsday*.

———. (2004, January 30). Jackson condemns media leaks.

———. (2004, December 31). Report: Martha Stewart loses decorating contest in prison.

———. (2005, March 11). Jackson story.

———. (2005, July 6). Martha Stewart calls house arrest "hideous." *LA Times*. Retrieved from www.latimes.com.

Ayres, D. (1997, January 26). Simpson trial: Closure, but for whom? *New York Times*.

Bachman, R. & L. Saltzman (1995, August). Violence against women: Estimates from the redesigned survey. *Bureau of Justice Statistics* (no. NCJ-154348). Washington, DC: U.S. Department of Justice.

Barak, G. (1994). Between the waves: Mass-mediated themes of crime and justice. *Social Justice, 21* (3), 133–147.

Barkan, S. (1997). Criminology: *A Sociological Understanding*. NJ: Prentice Hall

Bean, M. (2003, July 31). Court's lips are sealed for now. *Court TV*. Retrieved from www.courttv.com.

Bellamy, P. (n.d.). Retrieved from http://www.crimelibrary.com/notorious_murders/famous/ramsey/allegations_4.html

Beller, P. C. (2004, October 31). Pelosi trial: Not quite talk of the town. *New York Times*.

Bennett, L. (2000, November). *Globalization, media market reregulation and the future of public information*. Presented at the UNESCO-EU conference on The Global Public Sphere, The Media and the Information Society. Santiago de Compostela, Spain.

Bergen, R. K. (1999, March). Marital rape. *Violence Against Women Online Resources*. Retrieved April 18, 2001, from vaw.umn.edu/Vawnet/mrape.htm.

Bleick, E. (1995, October 23). Second time around—As the Menendez brothers once again fight for their lives, the prosecution alters its strategy. *Time*.

Bower, A. (2003, April 28). Murder in the family. *Time.*

Brennan, C. (1997, February 9). Ramsey case secrecy unusual. *Rocky Mountain News.*

Brenner, A. S. (2000). Cyber-rights and criminal justice: Legal resources on the web. Retrieved from http://avalon.caltech.edu/~thanne/law.html

Broder, J. M. (2004, January 14). From grand jury leaks comes a clash of rights. *New York Times.*

————. (2005, January 31). On eve of jury selection, Jackson begs for fair trial. *New York Times.*

————. (2005, February 25). Judge in Jackson case assures there is order in his court. *New York Times.*

Broder, J. M. & C. LeDuff. (2005, February 1). Jackson trial starts with fanfare and jury selection. *New York Times.*

Bruchey, S. (2003, October 28). Son's unanswered plea. *Newsday.*

————. (2004, September 20). Murder in the Hamptons. *Newsday.*

Bruchey, S. & R. Topping. (2004, November 11). Trial takes a mystical turn. *Newsday.*

Campos, P. (2005, May 3). The really important stuff. *Rocky Mountain News.* Retrieved from http://www.rockymountainnews.com/drmn/news_columnists/article/0,1299,DRMN_86_3746663,00.html

Center for Media and Public Affairs (1999). CMPA, 2100 L Street NW, Suite 300, Washington, DC 20037.

Cloud, J. (1998, May). *Time* online. Retrieved from www.time.com.

Clumsy Crooks. Funny real-life crime stories and pictures about dumb criminals. Retrieved February 15, 2004, from http://www.clumbsycrooks.com/caught.htm

Cohen, A. (2004, July 30). *CBS News.* Retrieved from www.CBSnews.com.

Cohen, J. (2005, May 6). Jackson's career won't survive trial. *Billboard.* Retrieved from http://www.billboard.com/bbcom/news/article_display.jsp?vnu_content_id=1000911902

Corliss, R. (2003, July 28). Say it isn't so, Kobe. *Time.*

————. (2003, December 1). The cuffed one. *Time.*

————. (2005, March 21). Jackson's bad day in court. *Time.*

Cottle, S. (1993). *TV news, urban conflict and the inner city.* London: Leicester University Press.

*Court TV Casefiles* (1997). Washington v. Mary Kay Letourneau. Retrieved online from http://www.courttv.com/archive/casefiles/verdicts/letourneau.html.

————. (1999). *Virginia v. Lorena Bobbitt.* Retrieved from http://www.courttv.com/archive/casefiles/verdicts/bobbitt.html.

Craven, D. (1996, December). Female victims of violent crime. *Bureau of Justice Statistics.* Retrieved April 5, 2001, from www.usdoj.gov.

Crawford, K. (2004, July 20). Martha: I cheated no one. CNN/Money. Retrieved from http://money.cnn.com/2004/07/16/news/newsmakers/martha_sentencing.

Crowley, K. (2005, April 6). Pelosi blows his deal plea. *New York Post* online edition.

————. (2005, May 5). Pelosi loses his temper. *New York Post* online edition.

Davis, F. J. (1953, June). Crime news in Colorado newspapers. *American Journal of Sociology* LVII, 325–330.

Dawson, J. & P. A. Langan (1994, July). Murder in families. *Bureau of Justice Statistics* (no. NCJ 143498). Retrieved April 11, 2001, from www.ojp.usdoj.gov.

Dershowitz, A. (1994). Did Virginia wife act in self defense? In *The abuse excuse and other cop-outs, sob stories, and evasions of responsibility.* Boston: Little, Brown.

Deutsch, L. (2004, December 16). Legal hotshot's star has fallen. *The Associated Press.*

Dinse, R. (2002, June 11). Retrieved from http://transcripts.cnn.com/TRANSCRIPTS/0206/11/lt.20.html

Dowdy, Z. R. (2005, May 5). Pelosi plea elicits three more years. *Newsday.*

Dowler, K. (2002). *Off Balance: Youth, Race & Crime in the News.* Berkeley Media Studies Group, Public Health Institute, Vincent Schiraldi, Justice Police Institute. April 2001.

Eftimiades, M. (1995). *Sins of the mother.* New York: St. Martin's Paperbacks.

Ehrenreich, B. (1994, July 18). Oh, those family values. *Time.*

Farley, M. & H. Barkan. (2001, April 16). Prostitution, violence against women, and posttraumatic stress disorder. *Prostitution Education Network* online.

Feinberg, S. (2002, Spring). Media effects: The influence of local newspaper coverage on municipal police size. *American Journal of Criminal Justice,* 26 (2).

Feinman, C. (1980). *Women in the criminal justice system.* New York: Praeger.

Fleeman, M. (2003, November). *Laci: Inside the Laci Peterson murder.* St. Martin's True Crime Library.

Forbes.com staff (2004, March 4). How Martha ended up in court. Retrieved from http://www.forbes.com/business/2004/03/04/cx_da_0304mstimeline.html

Fox, J. A. & M. W. Zawitz (2001, March). Homicide trends in the United States. *Bureau of Justice Statistics.* Retrieved from www.usdoj.gov.

Fox, R. & R. Van Sickel (2001). *Tabloid justice: Criminal justice in an age of media frenzy.* Lynne Rienner.

Gado, M. (2001, April 17). Pedophiles and child molesters: The slaughter of innocence. Retrieved from http://crimelibrary.com/serial/pedophiles.

Gainesvilletimes.com (2005, May 5). Opinion.

Gehring, K. (in press). In *Crime and the media: Headlines vs. reality,* eds. R. Muraskin & S. Feuer Domash, Upper Saddle River, NJ: Prentice Hall.

Geringer, J. (2001, April 15). Betty Broderick: Divorce...desperation...death. Retrieved from http://crimelibrary.com/classics2/broderick.

Gibbs, N. (1990, October 1). The hottest show in Hollywood. *Time.*

Gleick, E. (1995, October 23). Second time around—As the Menendez brothers once again fight for their lives, the prosecution alters its strategy. *Time.*

Graber, D. A. (1980). *Crime, news and the public.* New York: Praeger.

Greenfield, L. A. (1996, March). Child victimizers: Violent offenders and their victims. *Bureau of Justice Statistics* (no. NCJ-153258). Retrieved from www.ojp.usdoj.gov.

———. (1997, February). Sex offenses and offenders. Bureau of Justice Statistics (no. NCJ-163392). Retrieved from www.ojp.usdoj.gov.

Greenfield, L. A. & T. L. Snell (1999, December). Women offenders. *Bureau of Justice Statistics* (no. NCJ-175688). Retrieved from www.ojp.usdoj.gov.

Griffy, A. M. (2002). The media madness. Retrieved from http://www.justicejunction.com/innocence_lost_jonbenet_ramsey_media_madness.htm

Grossberg, J. (2004, June 25). Jackson judge dismisses media. *Time.*

Hamilton, M. (2003, March 27). The Elizabeth Smart case: Why we need specific laws against brainwashing. Retrieved from http://writ.news.findlaw.com/hamilton/20030327.html

Healy, P. (2004, October 14). Dead man's life comes under scrutiny at murder trial. *The New York Times.*

———. (2004, November 5). Now the Pelosi trial invokes a realm of the supernatural. *The New York Times.*

———. (2004, December 14). Pelosi guilty of murder of lover's husband in Hamptons. *The New York Times.*

Henderson, G. & R. Fields. (1994, November 4). Mother confesses to two boys' deaths. *The Herald-Journal* online.

Hochstetler, A. (2001). Reporting of executions in U.S. newspaper. *Journal of Cirme and Justice,* 24, 1.

Huff, R. (2005, May 10). Long Island murder to get an airing. *New York Daily News.*

Inciardi, J. & K. McElrath, eds. (2001). *The American drug scene: An anthology* (3rd. ed.). Roxbury.

Jenkins, P. (1999). *Synthetic panics: The symbolic politics of designer drugs.* New York University Press.

Jerin, R. & C. Fields (1994). Murder and mayhem in the USA today: A quantitative analysis of the reporting of state's news. In *Media, process and the social construction of crime: Studies in newsmaking criminology,* ed. G. Barak. New York: New Garland.

———. (2005). Murder and mayhem in the media: Media misrepresentation of crime and criminality. In *Visions for change: Crime and justice in the twenty-first century,* eds. R. Muraskin & A. Roberts. Upper Saddle River, NJ: Prentice Hall.

Johnson, K. (2004, August 27). In Bryant case, issues of power, not of race. *The New York Times.*

Jones, T. L. *Court TV.* Retrieved from www.crimelibrary.com.

Kappeler, V., M. Blumberg, & G. Potter (2000). *The mythology of crime and criminal justice* (3rd. ed.). Waveland Press.

Kass, J. (2004, September 3). Full court pressure avoided. *Newsday.*

Kelly, D. (2004, September 5). Town no longer in spotlight. *Newsday.*

Klite, P., R. A. Bardwell, & J. Salzman. (1997). Local TV news: Getting away with murder. *Press/Politics,* 2 (2), 102–112.

Knight, B. (2004, December). *Laci Peterson: The whole story.* iUniverse.

Koch, S. (1993, December 10). It's outrageous to blame me. *The New York Post.*

Kurtz, H. (2005, May 8). It's to laugh (or cry) about: Tragedy or farce? Either works for TV. *The Washington Post.* Retrieved from http://www.washingtonpost.com/wp-dyn/content/article/2005/05/07/AR2005050700153_pf.html

Lacayo, R. (1994, July 4). Playing to the crowd. *Time.*

Lafferty, E. (1997, February 17). The inside story of how O.J. lost the second time around. *Time.*

Langan, P. A. & J. M. Dawson (1995, September). Spouse murder defendants in large urban counties. *Bureau of Justice Statistics* (no. NCJ-153256). Retrieved from www.ojp.usdoj.com.

LeDuff, C. (2003, December 9). Official memo on Jackson casts doubt on charges. *The New York Times.*

Linder, D. O. A trial account. Retrieved from http://www.law.umkc.edu/faculty/projects/ftrials/Simpson/simpson.htm.

Lithwick, D. (2004, August 8). The shield that failed. *The New York Times.*

Liptak, D. (2005, March 30). Johnnie Cochran Jr., trial lawyer defined by O.J. Simpson case, is dead at 67. *The New York Times.*

MacDonald, E. (2004, February 4). Martha's little lies. *Forbes.* Retrieved from http://www.forbes.com/business/2004/02/04/cz_cm_0204martha.html

Macguire, K., et al. (1993). *Sourcebook of Criminal Justice Statistics, 1992.* Washington, DC: USGPO.

MacLeod, M. (2001, April 17). Aileen Wuornos: Killer who preyed on truck drivers. Retrieved from http://www.crimelibrary.com/serial4/wuornos/index.html

Madigan, N. & M. Sink (2004, September 3). End of Kobe Bryant case brings out strong sentiments. *The New York Times.*

Maloney, J. J. & P. O'Connor. (1999, May 7). The murder of JonBenet Ramsey. *Time.*

Manners, T. (1997). *Deadlier than the male: Stories of female serial killers.* London: Macmillan.

Marshall, C. (2004, November 13). Jury finds Scott Peterson guilty of wife's murder. *The New York Times.*

Mattingly, D. (2002, August 14). Missing kids: Has media coverage been fair? Retrieved from http://archives.cnn.com/2002/US/08/14/connie.missing.media/index.html

Mencken, H. L. (1926). *Prejudices, 5th series.* New York: Knopf.

Miller, M. C. (1998). *It's a crime: The economic impact of the local TV news in Baltimore—A study of attitudes and economics.* New York: Project in Media Ownership.

Molloy, T. (2005, May 8). Jackson defense will portray him as victim. *Newsday.*

Morin, R. (1997, August 18). An airwave of crime: While TV news coverage of murders has soared—feeding public fears—crime is actually down. *The Washington Post National Weekly Edition,* p. 34.

Moss, M. (1993, December 14). Editorial. *Newsday.*

Murphy, D. E. (2003, November 23). For lawyer, it's Michael Jackson on line 1, Scott Peterson on line 2. *The New York Times.*

———. (2004, June 2). Prosecutor outlines the case against Peterson. *The New York Times.*

Nash, R. (1982). *Wilderness and the American mind.* New Haven, CT: Yale University.

*Newsday.* Michael Jackson calls Santa Barbara County District Attorney Tom Sneddon a "cold man." (2003, November 21).

Newman, G. R. (1990). Popular culture and criminal justice: A preliminary analysis. *Journal of Criminal Justice,* 18, 261–274.

Newton, M. (2000). The encyclopedia of serial killers. New York: Checkmark Books, 242–245.

*New York Times* (2004, August 19). Cronkite decries TV News.

———. (2004, September 3). End of Kobe Bryant case brings out strong emotions.

Noe, D. (n.d.). Mary Kay Letourneau: The romance that was a crime. *Court TV.* Retrieved April 23, 2006, from http://www.crimelibrary.com/criminal_mind/psychology/marykay_letourneau/1.html.

Olsen, G. (1999). *If loving you is wrong.* New York: St. Martin's Paperbacks.

Pergament, R. (2001). Susan Smith: Child murderer or victim? *Court TV.* Retrieved April 5, 2001, from http://www.crimelibrary.com/fillicide/smith.

Pergament, R. (2003, November 11). The Menendez brothers. Retrieved from http://www.crimelibrary.com/notorious_murders/famous/menendez/

Potter, G. & V. Kappeler (2000). *Constructing crime: Perspectives on making news and social problems.* Long Grove, IL: Waveland Press.

Reinarman, C. & H. Levine (1997). *Crack in America: Demon drugs and social justice.* University of California Press.

Rennison, C. M. & S. Welchans (2000, May). Intimate partner violence. *Bureau of Justice Statistics* (no. NCJ-178247). Retrieved April 5, 2001, from www.ojp.usdoj.gov.

Ressner, J. (2005, February 14). The thriller begins. *Time.*

Reynolds, M. (2004). *Dead ends: The pursuit, conviction and execution of female serial killer Aileen Wuornos, the damsel of death.* New York: St Martin's Press.

Riley, J. (2005, January 30). King goes into court. *Newsday.*

Robinson, C. (1991). *California v. Broderick.* Betty Broderick on trial: Victim or criminal? *Court TV.*

Sacco, V. F. & M. Trotman (1990). Public information programming and family violence: Lessons learned from the mass media crime prevention experience. *Canadian Journal of Criminology,* 32 (1), 91–105.

Saporito, B. (2004, September 13). Kobe rebound. *Time.*

Schiller, L. & KLS Communications (1999, April). *Perfect murder, perfect town.* New York: HarperCollins.

Schlesinger, P., H. Tumber, & G. Murdock (1991). The media politics of crime and criminal justice. *British Journal of Sociology,* 42 (3), 397–420.

The Scopes "Monkey Trial"—July 10–25, 1925. Retrieved December 27, 2004, from http://www.dimensional. com/~randl/scopes.htm, pp. 1–13.

The Salem Witch Trials 1692: A Chronology of Events www.salemweb.com/memorial.

Searcey, D. (2005, March 7). The circus in Santa Maria. *Newsday.*

———. (2005, April 4). Milking Michael's misery. *Newsday.*

Sheley, J. F. & C. D. Ashkins (1981). Crime, crime news and crime views. *Public Opinion Quarterly,* 45, 492–506.

Smart, E. & L. Smart with L. Morton (2003). *Bringing Elizabeth home: A journey of faith and hope.* Doubleday.

Smart, T. & L. Benson (2005). *In plain sight: The startling truth behind the Elizabeth Smart investigation.* Chicago Review Press.

Snyder, H. N. (2000, July). Sexual assault of young children as reported to law enforcement: Victim, incident, and offender characteristics. *Bureau of Justice Statistics* (no. NCJ-182990). Retrieved April 5, 2001, from www.opj.usdoj.gov.

Song, S. (2005, January 26). Pretrial motions. *Time.*

Stanley, A. (2003, November 20). Stardom plus scandal in a shame-free age. *The New York Times.*

Sternheimer, K. (2005, May 15). The silence of the young. *Newsday.*

Stone, I. (1941). *Clarence Darrow for the defense.* Garden City, NY: Doubleday.

Stumbo, B. (1993). *Under the twelfth of never.* New York: Pocket Books/Simon & Schuster.

Surette, R. (1998). *Media, crime and criminal justice: Images and realities.* Pacific Grove, CA: Brooks/Cole.

Sussman, T. (2005, February 9). Conservatives who had tried for five years to pass the law. *Newsday.*

———. (2005, May 23). Simmering race issues. *Newsday.*

Taylor, C. (2004, June 14). Peterson's Martha defense. *Time.*

The Salem Witch Trials 1692: A chronology of events. http://www.salemweb.com/memorial.

Thomas, S. & D. Davis, (2000). *JonBenet: Inside the Ramsey murder investigation.* New York: St. Martin's Press.

*Time* (1995, January 24). O.J. Simpson...Will Ito ban TV coverage?

———. (1999, May). Modern public relations has come a long way since the days of "no comment."

*Time Magazine Notebook* (2005, January 26).

Ulick, J. (2003, June 4). Martha indicted, resigns. *CNNMoney.* Retrieved from http://money.cnn.com/2003/06/04/news/martha_indict.

*USA Today/CNN/Gallup Poll* (1993, October 28). Crime in America.

U.S. Department of Justice (1999). Murders and nonnegligent manslaughters known to police. Table. *Sourcebook of Criminal Justice Statistics* online. Retrieved from http://albany.edu/sourcebook.

———. (1999). Rate (per 1,000 females and males) of violent victimization. Table. *Sourcebook of Criminal Justice Statistics* online. Retrieved from http://albany.edu/sourcebook.

———. (1999). Victim and offender relationship in personal victimization. Table. *Sourcebook of Criminal Justice Statistics* online. Retrieved from http://albany.edu/sourcebook.

Van Biema, D. (1995, February 6). A fool for a client. *Time.*

Vasquez, B. (1997, August 15). PR pro Russell joins Ramseys' Camp. *The Denver Business Journal.* www.clumsycrooks.com/caught.htm.

Walsh, J. (1995, October 16). The lessons of the trial. *Time.*

Waxman, S. (2004, July 29). The trial outside the court. *The New York Times.*

Williams, L. (2005, April 6). Pelosi blows pleas. *Daily News.*

Wilson, N. K. (2002). Taming women and nature: The criminal justice system and the creation of crime in Salem Village. In *It's a crime: Women and justice,* ed. R. Muraskin. Upper Saddle River, NJ: Prentice Hall.

Winters, R. (2003, September 8). Where there's a will. *Time.*

Young, M. & P. Mintz. (2003, December 10). The race debate. *Newsday.*

Young, M. R. (2003, December 14). Gulotta takes his case to Stern. *Newsday.*

Zaret, E. (1997, January 18). Ramseys hire only the best. *Daily Camera.*

Zoglin, R. (2005, February 6, 14). Remember televised trials. *Time.*

# Index